Disenfranchised from America

*Reinventing Language and Love
in Nabokov and Pynchon*

Melissa Lam

University Press of America,® Inc.
Lanham · Boulder · New York · Toronto · Plymouth, UK

Copyright © 2009 by
University Press of America,® Inc.
4501 Forbes Boulevard
Suite 200
Lanham, Maryland 20706
UPA Acquisitions Department (301) 459-3366

Estover Road
Plymouth PL6 7PY
United Kingdom

All rights reserved
Printed in the United States of America
British Library Cataloging in Publication Information Available

Library of Congress Control Number: 2009924638
ISBN-13: 978-0-7618-4619-2 (paperback : alk. paper)
eISBN-13: 978-0-7618-4620-8

∞™ The paper used in this publication meets the minimum
requirements of American National Standard for Information
Sciences—Permanence of Paper for Printed Library Materials,
ANSI Z39.48-1992

Dedication

This book is dedicated to my grandmother who taught me how to read.

Hin Chun Lam

1912-2008

Contents

Preface	vii
Acknowledgments	ix
Introduction	xi

Section I: Lolita

1. Trickery and Linguistic Device	3
2. Freud and American Suburbia	7
3. Defamiliarization and Landscape	15
4. The Underworld: America as Movie	19
5. The Resuscitation of the Romance Genre	23
6. Defamiliarization and Language	29

Section II: The Crying of Lot 49

7. The Inside Outsider: Defamiliarization and the Narrator	41
8. Illegitimacy and Disruptive Imagination	47
9. W.A.S.T.E. Everywhere: Pynchon at the Movies	59
10. 'The Direct Apocalyptic Word': Defamiliarization and Bakhtin	71

Final Remarks	77
Bibliography	83
Index	87
About the Author	91

Preface

The research for this book began the day that I went to see a Romantic movie and realized that the majority of the audience in the theater was left unmoved by the film's cliché depictions of love. I began to pay closer attention to American depictions of love, hate, terror and tragedy in literature and cinema and realized that what worked best was the art form made strange. This book is a culmination of my investigation into these universal human matters and my findings.

Melissa Lam
Hong Kong
January 2009

ACKNOWLEDGEMENTS

This book would not have been possible without the help of the many who offered advice and close readings during these past 2 years. The finely honed rereadings of Mark Williams and Jed Mayer deserve mention right at the start. So too does Brian McHale, who has always been particularly insightful in his comments and has continued to inspire me as a mentor and friend. Thanks also to Brian Boyd and Leonard Wilcox who have played no small part in offering invaluable advice and criticism when most needed.
I am grateful to the University of Canterbury and Chinese University of Hong Kong, both institutions which have nurtured me and given me the financial support and necessary research assistance over the years. Thanks to the University Press of America, acquisitions editor Suzanne Kirk and my copy editor Emily Hewitt for having confidence in my work and being supportive of it. Lastly, thanks to my family, Rossana, Frank and Jonathan for their amazing patience and support.

Copyright © 1965, 1966 by Thomas Pynchon. Copyright Renewed 1993, 1994 by Thomas Pynchon. Reprinted by permission of HarperCollins Publishers.

From LOLITA by Vladimir Nabokov, copyright © 1955 by Vladimir Nabokov. Used by permission of Vintage Books, a division of Random House, Inc.

INTRODUCTION

THE DIALOGIC DISCOURSE

Eighty years ago William Carlos Williams wrote a poem entitled 'To Elsie'. The first two stanzas describe vast geography, a landscape encompassing an enormous range of 'mountain folk from Kentucky / or the ribbed north end of / Jersey' (3-5). The panoramic view of 'devil-may-care-men' railroading and 'young slatterns' flaunting, disappears in the second half of the poem when the general description of the American scene begins to shrink, and the focus shifts to one girl:

> sent out at fifteen to work in
> some hard-pressed
> house in the suburbs—
>
> some doctor's family, some Elsie—
> voluptuous water
> expressing with broken
>
> brain the truth about us (37-43).

This broken girl, this 'Elsie' concentrates the vast panorama of Williams' geographical description; the 'desolate' girl acts as a metonymy for America. Thirty years later, *Lolita* erupts onto the literary scene, disturbing the homogenizing culture of 1950s America. Written in 1955 by Russian émigré Vladimir Nabokov, the novel tells the tale of a pedophile and his thirteen-year-old American kidnappee who twice journey the entire expanse of America. We are lost in the cinematic descriptions of the environment but as in Williams' poem, Nabokov concentrates the narrative gaze onto the specific—Lolita/Dolores Haze is the main subject and incarnation of fallen America, the inescapable effects of tragedy and damage reflected back at the reader:

> In her washed-out gray eyes, strangely spectacled, our poor romance was for a moment reflected, pondered upon, and dismissed like a dull party, like a rainy picnic to which only the dullest bores had come, like a humdrum exercise, like a bit of dry mud caking her childhood (Nabokov 289).

Lolita is all flat-chested, big-footed, pre-teen goofiness when Humbert falls in love with her. Humbert pursues his passion avidly and Lolita's vulgar simplicity only helps to make her desirable. Humbert conceals this girlish ordinariness by initiating her into performing various sexual acts, her objections muted by the presence of our first person narrator. Through the voice of Humbert, Nabokov commentates throughout the novel on a society that manages to exude both vulgarity and innocence. This assessment of America is expressed in the description of cultural landscape, the play of interrelationships between watcher and watched, seducer and victim, as well as in the character of young Lolita.

In Thomas Pynchon's *The Crying of Lot 49*, Oedipa Maas feels driven to catalogue an insane world of debauchery, pop music, and baffling human behavior into a semblance of the Eisenhower world of suburban Kinneret she has left behind. The America of San Narciso is indecipherable to Oedipa; as she cannot 'measure its field strength' or 'count its line of force'—she finds herself a stranger in her own country (11). Oedipa's narrative consciousness amplifies abnormal events; she is an American insider who sees with the unsettling perspective of an outsider. Oedipa is an unreliable cryptologist, attempting to piece together 'signs' in the landscape into an elaborate plotted narrative of America: a mystery with a solution if only she can penetrate the code. However, her unfamiliar perspective ensures that instead of assembling puzzle pieces in a mystery she achieves the opposite, knitting larger complexities, and uncovering more confusing possibilities. As in Nabokov's *Lolita*, the narrator's preoccupation with strange or untoward images of the environment is caught up in an effort to explain their outsiderness to the society in which they find themselves.

This book examines the ways in which *Lolita* and *The Crying of Lot 49* defamiliarize our world and ways of thinking. Both novels use formal literary techniques to make ordinary cultural artifacts, situations, and environments seem unfamiliar from our every day perceptions. This process of defamiliarizing the regular and everyday has greater implications of estranging universal themes such as love, environment, and belonging. Both novels also question our precarious hold on corporeality by interpreting plot through two outside narrators whose trustworthiness is constantly placed in doubt. *Lolita* and *The Crying of Lot 49* unsettle the categories of truthfulness and reinvention in their interpretations of America's immediate cultural and environmental landscape. Both texts blur the distinction between recorded and imaginatively reconstructed worlds: just so, America isolates our two narrators in the text from their immediate landscape.

Both Nabokov and Pynchon have a preoccupation with the idea of the 'outsider' in American society, and their novels are frequently situated around an excommunicated member of the community. Because of their marginalized position, the outsider is able to maintain an ironic critical distance when commenting on their mass cultural environment. Interloper Humbert travels America cleverly disguised as an insider to allow his trespass across the country with his nymphet. Oedipa's housewife occupation and citizenship mark her as a native, but her observations and experiences are those of a foreigner entering an unknown country. *Lolita* and *Lot 49* are filtered through what Nabokov refers to as 'the sifting agent': a focus of consciousness through which other characters, situations and environments are seen.[1]

What is considered by most of society as familiar is made unfamiliar through the alienated perspectives of the outsider narrators in these two novels. In both texts, cultural distortion, uncanny repetition, and a fascination with the cinematic foster the sense of strangeness in the American landscape. This strangeness filters into the written and spoken language of post-war American society, even that of the lapsed world of commerce, advertising and motel names. Both Humbert and Oedipa distinctly narrate from an outsider's role, and both Nabokov and Pynchon use their manic odysseys as occasions to show off the riotous, extravagant possibilities of the English language that they have appropriated for their studies in America's 'craziness'.

The reader is invested in, even made complicit with the central narrative consciousness found in both texts. This beguiling consciousness however, is revealed to be untrustworthy—Humbert simultaneously protesting his guilt and innocence, and Oedipa's voice often confusingly interrupted by that of an additional narrator. Both *Lolita* and *Lot 49* undermine conventional techniques in fiction. In 'Slow Learner' Pynchon discusses constraints in his writing, noting that he felt in the early 1960s, 'a tendency to self-censorship' (*Short Stories*, 6). *Lot 49* was one of his first stabs at seriously playing with these boundaries, challenging fictional techniques and yet allowing an empathetic and aesthetically fluid voice to break through: 'begin [ning] to get a glimpse of how it was done' (23). In studying these novels, we are involved in an unsettling, even at times an estranging of our usual patterns of following a plot. In this book I examine the ways in which both of these authors use techniques that subvert readerly expectation to expose the hidden nature of an object or event and dismantle habitual perceptions.

Structural aspects of fiction which are defamiliarized (such as genre, landscape, and language) contribute to the feeling of strangeness, reflected in the language used by both writers. My critical approach is drawn from a number of sources, synthesized from the school of Russian Formalism—more specifically, Shklovsky's theory of 'Defamiliarization' defined as 'mak[ing] the familiar seem strange' (13). In 'Art as Technique', Shklovsky uses 'Defamiliarization' as a structural literary technique to counter familiarity and habit in artistic perception. He argues that familiarity with the same images and the same interpretation of emotions breeds complacency and a lazy eye as 'the over-automatization of an object permits the greatest economy of perceptive effort' (12). One of his more well-known passages states:

> The purpose of art is to impart the sensation of things as they are perceived and not as they are known. The technique of art is to make objects 'unfamiliar', to make forms difficult, to increase the difficulty and length of perception because the process of perception is an aesthetic end in itself and must be prolonged (12).

What Shklovsky means by this is that the less effort one uses to see everyday objects, the more intangible their existence. In everyday perceptions, objects appear to us as if 'they were enveloped in a sack', with only the faintest silhouette of the object visible (11). With our habitual manner of seeing images, we only register with minimal cognition in daily life. Defamiliarization challenges our expectations, producing an image untoward and alien to everyday awareness. Techniques used to achieve this include: narration from an outsider or unexpected consciousness,[2] placing unexpected metaphors together to create strange imagery, and the text being conscious of itself as a literary device, or artifice. The latter technique is often described as the essence of 'literariness', and is very similar with what is more commonly referred to as 'Metafiction': when fiction decides to bare its techniques and starkly reveal itself as artifice. These main techniques of defamiliarization are all used in *Lolita* and *Lot 49* in creative and imaginative ways by the authors to induce new perceptions and reevaluations of our commonly held beliefs.

Humbert's defamiliarization of Lolita and America allows us to view both subjects in purely aesthetic terms, forgoing our familiar values. In response to the controversial backlash against *Lolita*'s first printing, Nabokov ensnares us further, responding in his Afterword (added in 1956), that '*Lolita* has no moral in tow', only existing to afford 'aesthetic bliss' (332). Overtly, Humbert's confessions in *Lolita* concern his physical abuse of a twelve-year-old girl, but covertly the tale is about the reinvention of Dolores Haze and America into a wholly more strange and fantastic reality. Rubbish-littered gas stations are transformed into glittering Meccas, which Julia Bader refers to as Humbert's 'quasi-realistic American setting' (54). Commonplace pre-teen Dolores Haze is transformed into a striking vision—almost like a movie star—and the suburban environment is filled 'with awe and delight (the king crying for joy, the trumpets blaring, the nurse drunk)' (41). Humbert the outsider's governing perspective and means of infiltrating the community converts Ramsdale suburbia into a 'fantastic' neighborhood—the everyday is no longer habitual and normal, and the ordinary begins to seem strange.

This book contains two sections, each examining in turn the use of defamiliarization in *Lolita* and *Lot 49*. These two novels have also been chosen for discussion due to the compatibility of their linear timeframe when read together. *Lolita* is very much a novel of the 1950s and *Lot 49* (as Petillon argues), not a 60s novel but on the cusp of cultural change which manifested the craziness of the 1960s (129). Both texts explore particular idioms, slang, and verbal mannerisms that are central to understanding the changes affecting American language and culture in the decades following the Second World War. These linguistic changes are frequently drawn from cinematic influences, television, and advertisements.

Several key concepts will be used to further clarify and discuss the overarching theme of defamiliarization and its applicable supporting theories in respect to both texts. In Chapter Two, the strangeness of suburban neighborhood will be discussed in terms of Freud's 'Unheimlich' theory, which he refers to as 'the opposite of *heimlich* ['homely'], or *heimisch* ['native'], which is contrary to what is familiar' (54). The Unheimlich or the Uncanny is a term or literary concept used to explain a strange and untoward feeling in the environment that the narrator suddenly feels aware of. I will be using Anneleen Masschelein's interpretation of Freud's concept explaining 'Heim' as the German word for home, denoting feelings of comfort and familiarity. When such feelings become 'Unheim' the familiar is transformed into the unfamiliar. Masschelein's interpretation of 'The Uncanny' has clear associations with the principles of defamiliarization as both are occupied with the idea of the familiar becoming untoward or strange. The 'Heim'/ 'Unheim' dichotomy is projected onto the suburban neighborhood in *Lolita* and the census tract districts of *Lot 49*.

The third and seventh chapters of this book will discuss how cultural landscape in both texts evokes a high artificiality that is manifested in the American language. In *Lolita*, motel names such as 'Sunset Motels, U-Beam Cottages, and Hillcrest Courts' emphasize the kitsch nature of advertising language, and demonstrate how America's natural geographical landscape is replaced. Lolita and Humbert drive through a country in which this advertising landscape is placed at the forefront and natural scenery holds second place. In *Lot 49*, Oedipa is unable to think amidst the 'contemplative contours of residential streets', feeling more at ease in the 'freeway madness of an L.A. highway' (79). The concept of artificially constructed landscapes inducing self-alienation will be considered in relation to the simulated cinematic language spoken by both characters in the texts. This is manifested in an America where reality is constantly being measured against the seductive simulacra of film. Discontinuity techniques in fiction are further explored, focusing on Bakhtin's critical theories. These revolutionized our ideas about the language of literary texts that could no longer be viewed as monolithic, but as multifarious, with several voices, disruptions, and countervoices. These ideas of linguistic defamiliarization are present as 'heteroglossia' in *Lolita* and as 'dual voice narration' in *Lot 49*.

The final chapter reminds us of the convoluted nature of both texts and how difficult it is to constrain either of these author's novels within a particular category or genre. Deconstructing either text is also problematic, as the labyrinthine natures of both novels oblige us to reread again and again. *Lot 49* and *Lolita* are chosen for their different approaches to defamiliarization that unsettle us or their ability to reveal the unexpected or forgotten image in the ordinary. Shklovsky refers to this as 'chang[ing] its form without changing its nature' (13). He gives us a case in point that 'Greek architecture is considered a classical icon of structural beauty, yet not a single column of a Greek temple stands exactly in its proper order' (24). Shklovsky observes that there is similar disruption in novels where 'disordered rhythm' necessary to construct the aesthetics of beauty (24). In *Lolita* and *Lot 49*, it is this disruption of order and questioning of the limitations of fictional techniques that defamiliarize our understanding, 'increas[ing] the difficulty and length of perception' (Shklovsky, 12). This causes us to redefine ourselves as readers, as well as to forge a new awareness of the imaginative terrain we have entered.

My intention is to explore the ways in which these two authors manipulate the fictional strategies of a novel and defamiliarize our perceptions of everyday objects and people. Estranging our regular everyday perceptions allows us to more pertinently and intensely examine the critical issues of morality and identity that have become exhausted with over-examination to the point of cliché. *Lolita* preoccupies us with issues of morality, but the text also brings into question the nature of love, and whether it is possible in our modern era replete with self-conscious irony to reinvent it and make it new again. Nabokov takes us to extremes in *Lolita* where the most cherished and romantic of human emotions is brought to life again in the passions of a pedophile for his stepdaughter whom he rapes twice a day, every day, for two years. The book exudes love, but also death, and romance, famously with Nabokov's self-proclaimed love affair with the American language. This erudition is what makes Humbert's love so convincing—the manner in which America is both romanticized and exposed through a process of estranging our normal perceptions, thorough extraordinary language. In the same vein, *Lot 49* compels us to re-register reality through a series of eye-opening guises and events that are potent with meaning but leave us estranged, full of unanswered questions and doubts. Pynchon challenges Oedipa's claims about America, just as Nabokov interrogates Humbert's trespass and love of that 'lovely, trustful, dreamy, enormous country' which he has 'defiled with a sinuous trail of slime' (186). These novels both reexamine America through an unfamiliar perspective to allow us as readers to view it anew, interrogating our own relationships towards such clichéd loyalties as love, belonging, national identity, and finding a sense of place or meaning for ourselves in the world.

1. Nabokov explains the meaning of this term in his *Lectures on Literature* given at Cornell University, specifically discussing Jane Austen's *Mansfield Park*.

2. Shklovsky uses Tolstoy's story 'Kholstomer' as an example (13). The narrative consciousness is given from the horse's point of view as an example of defamiliarized technique. *Lolita* and *The Crying of Lot 49* also demonstrate this technique with both texts being narrated from an outsider's perspective.

SECTION ONE

LOLITA

'Lolita is not about sex but about love'

-Lionel Trilling

CHAPTER ONE

TRICKERY AND LINGUISTIC DEVIANCE

In 1940 Denis de Rougemont argued in *Love in the Western World* that narratives of romantic love drew their strength from some variety of social conflict and that in the modern era, pedophilia and incest were the only remaining taboos available to generate this (34). Six decades later, while sexual mores in the West have in general relaxed, child abuse has become the defining sexual crime and those who practice it the universally despised criminals. So how does one, over sixty years later come to terms with a novel that presents such loathsome subject matter in polished prose, through a highly refined consciousness? *Lolita* manages to seduce as well as repulse, making it this dichotomy between attraction and repulsion that one must still come to terms with over fifty years since the novel appeared, years in which *Lolita* has become canonical, recognized as the pivotal novel in the career of a writer, whom many scholars claim was one of the greatest authors writing in the English language.

Nabokov scholar Brian Boyd suggested that *Lolita* 'will never cease to shock' (227). Yet the shock of the book is not a function of the relative degrees of antagonistic public attention directed at its central subject. The book shocks because the reader is ushered into the mind of a child-rapist and finds there, not a monster, but a human being with tastes, sentiments and even sympathies. We must struggle to disentangle ourselves from that bullying, seductive mind, wrapped in rich metaphorical language. Moreover, we are continually disconcerted by the ways in which Humbert's narration makes strange the world it represents, disorienting our perceptions of the normal. Nabokov defamiliarizes America through Humbert's arch language, creating a permissible reality that allows room for his transgressive desires. In *Lolita*, structural aspects of defamiliarization are developed; firstly, through the transformation of small town suburbia into an uncanny world, and secondly, by the remaking of a familiar American landscape into an escapist cinematic frontier. The novel contains American language that is archly masked and reinvented. The characters are given voices which suggest their real desires only by way of gaps in the personal narration of a child abuser. Humbert's command of the English language, his succinct knowledge of American idioms and arch metaphor is unsurpassed. In *Lolita* however, this erudite prose is coupled with juvenile slang, kitsch cultural artifacts and the smuttiest of storylines. Humbert translates the American landscape through the romantic tropes he self-consciously employs into something unfamiliar, and thereby removed, from the world of ordinary judgment. Just so, he translates Dolores into an imaginary child of his superior imagination where her ravishment is no longer subject to normal moral disapproval. His extraordinary rendition of a quotidian world produces one not merely imaginative, but deliberately constructed, out of the conventional romantic and pop-cultural tropes of natural experience. This chapter is concerned with the processes in which Humbert defamiliarizes America and reinvents the country and the girl into something wholly magical and different in order to enact his morally repugnant desires. Examination of the technical aspects of defamiliarization and discussion of the narrative organization of *Lolita* will reveal how this text has continued to elicit such unexpected and unusual responses from his critics and readers.

Nabokov has cast Humbert as an outsider—he only arrives in America a third of the way into the text with the novel's setting already established as 'uncanny' even before he reaches his Lolita. Nabokov has already projected such fantastic settings and images in the first 50 pages as Humbert's ex-wife Valeria and her new husband on all fours eating bananas in a scientific experiment, a failed artic expedition in Canada where Humbert is acting psychiatrist, and a gay bachelorhood in France with a nymphet prostitute. In all of these previous situations, Humbert is already cast in the outsider's role—cuckolded husband, behavioral analyst, skulking John—putting him in the perfect position to critique America as a European outsider, disdainfully commenting on the vulgar commercial culture of America and her citizens. In *Lolita*, we have unforgettable examples of Humbert's making fun of the 'Hardware and Co. Calendar and cute breakfast nook' (81), 'Colonial Inns' which promised 'unlimited quantities of M-m-m food' (155), as well as 'Tourist homes' which the narrator sneeringly calls 'country cousins of Funeral ones' (154). Americans are described in turn as 'stinking high school boys' (155), 'mummy necked farmer(s)' (161), 'inept waiters (ex-convicts or college boys)' (163-4), 'goons in luxurious cars,' and 'maroon morons near blued pools' (168). Humbert's incessant criticism of American culture masks the squalid nature of his purpose: in demeaning America he elevates his desires. The other characters are rarely able to speak in a voice that is not mimicked and are therefore silenced. The most glaring omission of these voices is twelve-year-old Dolores Haze, whose personality and physical characteristics are known to us only through the shuttered lens of the narrator. Humbert's reinvention of both Dolores and America creates a different, more fantastic country imposed on a real one. Dolores becomes Lolita—no longer a real girl—and Humbert is no longer a transgressor in terms he allows us to relate to any recognizable reality. Humbert is adept at reinvention, describing himself early on as 'a great big handsome hunk of movieland manhood' (41), setting up his story with the notion cunningly inserted into the reader's mind that he has 'all the characteristics which, according to writers on the sex interests of children, start the responses stirring in a little girl: clean-cut jaw, muscular hand, deep sonorous voice, broad shoulder. Moreover [he is] said to resemble some crooner or actor chap on whom Lo has a crush' (45). An uncanny representation of America is filtered through Humbert's refined consciousness. In *Lolita,* the storyline of the mismatched couple is developed through this very technique of reinventing Americans and making America strange.

CHAPTER TWO

FREUD AND AMERICAN SUBURBIA

Humbert first presents Dolores Haze/ Lolita to us in her most congenial environment, the Haze home piazza where she is 'half naked, kneeling', lying on a mat 'in a pool of sun' (41). Nabokov's strategies of Defamiliarization are interestingly pinpointed here, corresponding with Shklovsky's methods of making the commonplace unfamiliar, 'mak[ing] forms difficult, and increas[ing] the difficulty and length of perception' (12). An uncanny environment is created in Ramsdale, an ordinary American suburb in the Eastern United States and the once familiar environment for our Dolores Haze. Abnormalcy is established in Humbert's repulsion, juxtaposed with his immediate embrace—when he transposes his memory of Annabel from his European boyhood onto Dolores—towards suburban culture.[1] Humbert's repulsion is ostensible in his initial inspection of the Haze house. Such items as an old gray tennis ball, a brown apple core, bedraggled magazines, limp wet 'things' over the dubious tub divulge expected squalor, and as Boyd notes, 'only [confirm] his fastidious disgust' (235). This initial abhorrence is confronted with immediate familiarity in the 'piazza,' as Humbert transposes the memory of Annabel from his European boyhood, onto Dolores. Ramsdale, a typical middle class American suburb, is immediately presented as a 'weird' and 'uncanny' environment. The spookiness of the neighborhood evokes Freud's 'Uncanny,' an explanation of eerie and unaccountable strangeness in atmosphere. 'Unheimlich,' according to Freud,[2] is associated with strangeness, unfamiliarity and eeriness. More specifically, Freud designates the 'Uncanny' as nothing new and foreign in the environment but like Shklovsky's 'Defamiliarization' stemming from the familiar perceived as strange. Anneleen Masschelein's 'A Homeless Concept,' interprets Freud's 'Uncanny' as 'Heim' (or home), having two very distinct meanings that work in opposition to each other. The first meaning is straight-forward, home is construed as a safe place, where one finds familiar rest in an intimate setting. Charlotte welcoming Humbert as a close member of the family is a good example of this uncomplicated meaning of home. The second meaning of 'Heim' is more sinister, and gestures towards the hidden quality of a secret, something clandestine. Masschelein convincingly argues that this complicates the notion of 'Heim' or 'Home' when we consider 'Unheim' or 'Unheimlich' (The Uncanny). These uneasy feelings are prevalent from the moment Humbert steps off the train and into Ramsdale. 'Unheimlich' is applicable to Humbert's arrival in America as the stable familial 'home' he expects to be welcomed into, is instead a chaotic ruin destroyed by a house fire. The idea of 'coming home' is traditionally associated with returning to the normal, or reverting to the familiar and comforting. Humbert assumes certain preconceived notions about the concept of heim/home in an American suburban middle-class neighborhood. These assumptions collapse once Humbert actually arrives in America. Humbert's description of Ramsdale is filled with strange imagery, transforming the American suburb into the opposite of its originally signified meaning.

Humbert's new American heim/homeland is closer to Masschelein's second, more sinister definition of Heim, or even 'Unheimlich.' The second definition of 'Heim' and the antonym 'Unheimlich' are very similar in meaning, collapsing the distinction between both words (Masschelein, 'A Homeless Concept'). Masschelein interprets Freud's essay thus: 'the specificity of the sensation of the Uncanny lies in the fact that something is frightening, not because it is unfamiliar or new, but because what used to be familiar has somehow become strange.' Humbert's arrival in a familiar American home immediately casts Ramsdale under an auspicious note of 'unfamiliarity.' Humbert is driven into his suburban stalking ground in a stretch limo almost running over a dog (Charlotte's dying in this manner will later jolt the reader backwards in a fantastic déjà vu). His arrival in an untypical stretch limo creates disjuncture between quiet expectations of entering a familiar 'Heim,' and the foreigner conspicuously introduced. This formal entrance also emphasizes the contrast when a few short months later he drives the family sedan down the same road, disguised as an insider.

Lolita's second major suburban passage also evokes the Heim/Unheim dichotomy. Increasing queerness is noted in the sequence of events leading to Humbert and Charlotte's marriage. The narrative becomes dramatically stranger with Humbert's reading of Charlotte's confession of love to him and, at first glance, mistaking the childish nature of the scrawl for Lolita's writing (71). The descriptive passage of the suburban neighborhood is conveyed through the lens of an intoxicated Humbert who decides to mow the lawn:

> I decided to busy myself with our unkempt lawn. *Une petite attention.* It was crowded with dandelions, and a cursed dog—I loathe dogs—had defiled the flat stones where a sundial had once stood. Most of the dandelions had changed from suns to moons. The gin and Lolita were dancing in me and I almost fell over the folding chairs that I attempted to dislodge. Incarnadine zebras! There are some eructations that sound like cheers—at least, mine did (76).

Humbert's drunkenness disorients the reader and attaches a lurid quality to his actions. The unusual metaphors he uses to describe ordinary suburban artifacts, contribute to the queerness in the passage. The dandelions are not weeds but 'suns and moons.' Folding chairs are not furniture but 'zebras' (76). Even the noise of his belching is not natural bodily gas, but referred to in words of applause and jubilation. Humbert is mowing the lawn—a paternal chore he defamiliarizes with his drunken, predatory glances at the neighborhood girls. He also hides behind the lawnmower, a suburban technology that allows him to fit successfully into the neighborhood. The success of his ploy transforms an ordinary object into an alien artifact. Humbert takes a routine paternal chore and makes it strange by employing it as pretence of American normality.[3] Suburban machines such as the lawnmower and the family sedan are all trappings that constitute the American suburban 'Dad' whom Humbert disguises himself as successfully. Humbert's success at aping this role defamiliarizes its familiar and habitual nature.

The rest of Humbert's description of Ramsdale suburbia is conveyed to the reader in patterns of light and shade. Humbert keeps an eye on the section of the street where Charlotte's car will eventually appear, through the blinding gaze of 'bits of grass optically twittering in the low sun' (77). He watches two little girls playing on the street 'both talking at the top of their sunny voices,' the prettier of the two characterized by 'her bright hair' (77). These girls are eclipsed from Humbert's 'Green Goat' gaze by the shadow and property of 'Mr. and Mrs. Humbert's residence' (77). Humbert surveys the scene through a filtered lens of drunkenness; he sees a station wagon covered in leaves driving down the street 'before the shadows snapped,' and it is revealed not to be 'Mrs. Humbert' driving home, but 'the sweatshirted driver, roof-holding with his left hand and the junkman's dog tearing alongside' (77). Humbert's gaze surveys, directed and redirected by the movement of light and shade on the street. This gives the scene an unfamiliar and strange feeling. Humbert's actions (drunk and mowing the lawn), as well as the cold observation of each individual's actions on the street, contribute to the aberrant environment. The little girls, Negro chauffeur, and the sweat-shirted driver are delineated as bizarre apparitions rather than ordinary citizens. These suburbanites are made strange with the addition of the interloper's gaze, evaluating and assessing their significance. Humbert's addition to the quiet American suburb has made everything common and conventional seem contrived and fantastic. This is made more atypical by nobody in the neighborhood recognizing him as an interloper, even though he is drunk, erratically mowing the lawn. The usual pictorial scene of a father mowing the lawn, skipping children, and a dog barking at a car takes on a bizarre quality, viewed through the lens of an outsider. All the elements of a familiar 'heim' become unfamiliar with the addition of Humbert Humbert, naturally fitting in yet rendering everything uncanny by his very ease of disguise.

In the Ramsdale suburbia section, Nabokov shows how Humbert's culture of perversion infiltrates the sphere of suburban domesticity in America. As Marling illustrates, this is a world substantiated in popular 1950s family shows such as *Tea for Two (1950)*, *Father Knows Best (1951)*, and *I Love Lucy (1952)*, all expounding the virtues of a cohesive family unit individuals return to in order to solve their conflicts (4-5).[4] In *Lolita,* conflict of interest and domestic drama in the Haze household are solved by Humbert's marrying Charlotte and creating a stable suburban unit. Humbert takes advantage of these domestic conceits structuring the dominant representations of normalcy, and uses them to his advantage. In Ramsdale, we have a conscious parody of American suburban life, coldly assessed and participated in by our narrator. Once Humbert, (the outside element) becomes a part of this suburban 'heim,' he transforms it into an 'unheim,' generating an uneasy environment. Humbert manipulates preconceived notions of American father and home, to allow room for him to realize his fantastic desire of possessing Dolores Haze. His interloper status is unnoticed by the rest of the characters in Ramsdale who are blind to his perverse presence in their world. Humbert's previous history of unnoticed perversity and alienness supports the same degree of acceptance in America. Stark believes that Humbert's sexual perversion acts as a metaphor for his outsider presence, 'symboliz[ing] the alien's loneliness' (104). He characterizes Humbert as an outsider who 'desire[s] sexual objects' that he has trouble attaining, and thus isolating oneself 'just as the alien inevitably lives to some extent in isolation' (104). Stark's argument is strongly contextualized when we remember that Humbert's desire for nymphets was present before his move to America; voicing pedophilic desires during his first marriage to Valeria, buying young prostitutes in France, even eyeing young Eskimos during the strange Canadian Artic Expedition. In each previous environment, Humbert is illustrated in an outsider's role—he is the cuckolded husband, the slinking John—and tellingly in Canada, he is the social psychologist, responsible for cataloguing and observing the rest of the group's behavior with an outsider's eye.

The two suburban passages end with a final portraiture Humbert conceives for us moments before Charlotte's death. Driving home from the doctor's office, Humbert conveys a wholly different mood from the drunken lumbering of the previous suburban portrait. He is finally blending in and begins to experience contentment in American provincialism.

> I left in great spirits. Steering my wife's car with one finger, I contentedly rolled homeward. Ramsdale had, after all, lots of charm. The cicadas whirred; the avenue had been freshly watered. Smoothly, almost silkily, I turned down into our steep little street. Everything was somehow so right that day. So blue and green. I knew the sun shone because my ignition key was reflected in the windshield; and I knew it was exactly half past three because the nurse who came to massage Miss Opposite every afternoon was tripping down the narrow sidewalk in her white stockings and shoes. As usual, Junk's hysterical setter attacked me as I rolled downhill, and as usual, the local paper was lying on the porch where it had just been hurled by Kenny.
>
> The day before I had ended the regime of aloofness I had imposed upon myself and now uttered a cheerful homecoming call as I opened the door of the living room... (100-101).

The final suburban scene is framed with a pictorial 'blue and green,' as if in a color magazine advertisement. The sun is shining, the lawns are freshly watered. Humbert enters the Haze's home uttering a 'cheerful homecoming call,' eerily reminiscent of the role of the 1950s American father, coming home from work and announcing his paternal presence in the home (Marling 129). In the three portrait-like suburban scenes in *Lolita*, the first two scenes illuminate Ramsdale's gradual defamiliarization in which Humbert is instrumental in reassessing the normal into the unfamiliar, as well as acting as the foreign element that invades society. Humbert feels comfortable in Ramsdale in this final suburban scene; he is driving home cheerfully, convinced that he is successfully disguised in his role of small town husband. Everything is familiar to him now; he turns down the street 'smoothly; almost silkily' (100). Humbert reinforces the veracity of his claims with such sentences as 'I knew the sun shone because...' and 'I knew it was exactly half past three because...' Sentences like, '...as usual, Junk's hysterical setter attacked me,' and 'as usual, the local paper was lying on the porch,' also reiterate familiarity juxtaposed with the strangeness of the previous two suburban scenes. Humbert is driving home in a relaxed manner, one finger casually steering his wife's car. His fraudulent role as husband has become almost natural to him and, arriving at the Haze homestead, opens the door 'uttering a cheerful homecoming call' (101). Nabokov reinforces Humbert's familiarity by the sudden interposition, 'everything was somehow so right that day' (100). Humbert consciously plays the role of suburban father and, even though he is enjoying the ruse, it is not a natural feeling but a calculated one. His overt familiarity in Ramsdale does a thorough job of making everyday cultural artifacts strange in their normalized setting. In his portrayal of Humbert the suburban father, Nabokov disorientates and lulls with the comforting suburban scenes, yet also repulses by creating easy sympathy with our outside narrator.

Nabokov sets up deliberate similarities in the background of these three suburban scenes in order to emphasize subtle but crucial differences. In an attempt to minimize confusion, I have named the three suburban scenes for discussion as 'Arrival,' 'Resolve,' and 'Betrayal.' 'Arrival' in Ramsdale constitutes the first suburban scene, the second scene (mowing the lawn) involves Humbert's euphoric 'Resolve' to marry Charlotte for Dolores, and the third scene deals with Charlotte's discovery ('Betrayal') and her subsequent death. Nabokov structures these three scenes with key similarities—each scene has Humbert operating or involved with technological apparatuses (limousine, lawn mower, family sedan). These consumer machines are cultural suburban artifacts that signify family (car) or contrast with (the limo) American middle-class life. Miss Opposite's homestead is also mentioned in each scene, with a comment about her staff (the grinning Negro, the punctual nurse), ending with an exasperated acknowledgement of the barking dog. Ending the passage with the dog slyly completes the suburban family portrait. In 'Arrival,' Humbert is driven down the street in an old limousine, an obvious interloper and oddity in relation to the middle-class suburban neighborhood. 'Resolve' does not have him in the vehicle, but operating a lawnmower behind the house and spying with a sense of paranoia. These two scenes are in stark contrast with 'Betrayal,' where familiarly 'steering my wife's car with one finger,' Humbert 'contentedly roll[s] homeward' before cheerfully shouting out a greeting at the Ramsdale home (100). The freshly watered lawn that he drives past in 'Betrayal' is reminiscent of the 'Resolve' scene of the grass 'optically glimmering' at him and his struggle to mow the unkempt lawn. 'Arrival' has Humbert cautiously and distastefully entering the Haze home, noting nothing but imperfections amid the bourgeois banality of the house. 'Betrayal' has him rightfully bursting in as owner into the Haze home, uttering a cheerful husbandly call of welcome to his wife, feeling that 'everything was somehow so right that day.' Nabokov tellingly has Charlotte wearing the same outfit she wore the first time she met him to emphasize the structural recapitulation of this final suburban scene (100).

By creating structural similarities in the three main suburban scenes in Part One, Nabokov demonstrates the infiltration of Humbert into American suburbia, employing his very success to render the neighborhood atmosphere strange. The small American suburb becomes defamiliarized firstly through an outsider's infiltration, secondly, through the same outsider's critical assessing gaze. Humbert's irony and critical distance grants him a great deal of control over what he observes in the cultural landscape. This calculating eye is a major source of unsettlement and Humbert is always an outsider, trying to account for its difference and the unsettling qualities that this produces. In Chapter Three, we see this unsettling environment more aptly explored as Humbert and Dolores complete their transcontinental journey across America.

Notes

1. The mixture of attraction and repulsion he feels are both represented by Dolores Haze.

2. Masschlein's concept of 'heim' and 'unheim' is interpreted from Sigmund Freud's 1918 'Unheimlich' essay.

3. This pretence of normality is further intensified when Humbert is driving the family sedan home. The 1950s, as Karal Ann Marling notes, was the beginning of autoeroticism with the father driving home the family sedan from work. Please see chapter 5 'Autoeroticism: America's love affair with the car in the Television Age' for more information (128).

4. For more on 1950s family values regimented on television see Alan Nadel's *Containment Culture*.

CHAPTER THREE

DEFAMILIARIZATION AND LANDSCAPE

Nabokov chooses two benchmarks of American landscape to defamiliarize in *Lolita*: the suburban landscape as well as the larger and more general 'American outdoors'. 'Uncanniness' is manifested in the erudite descriptions of landscape, where America itself—its physical space—is made strange. In Ramsdale, Humbert ghoulishly plays a suburban father completing household chores. His narrative however, betrays his contempt, as Humbert repeatedly mocks Charlotte's home-decorating infatuation and Lolita's comic book and movie fixation. In a particularly cutting example, he derisively describes Charlotte finding her new husband's face comparable in beauty to the reflection of nature on her refrigerator[1] (81). This dynamic between American appropriations of natural landscape filtered through artificial means is aptly demonstrated in the second section of the novel as Dolores and Humbert journey across America. In *Lolita*, there are different orders of strangeness that develop as the novel progresses. Humbert defamiliarizes conventional America, but Nabokov illustrates how natural American landscape is made uncanny through the commercial appropriation of cinema and advertising. This transmogrified landscape is commented on and further filtered through the consciousness of Humbert the outsider. In addition to this, Humbert not only notices the unsettling environment, but admits that his interloper presence further corrupts the landscape, leaving a 'sinuous trail of slime across that lovely, trustful, dreamy, enormous country' (186). The estranging of naturalness into artificiality is one of Shklovsky's key examples of literary defamiliarization (Lemon, 4).

Humbert defamiliarizes a country already made strange by the filtrations of its landscape and social forms in a ubiquitous popular culture. He details lists of motels—Sunset, U-beam, HillCrest, Pine View, Skyline, Park Plaza, Green Acres (154)—all containing signifiers of natural landscape. Actual natural landscapes are never 'natural' but infused with cinematic imagery. Barbara Wyllie has devoted an entire book to this subject in *Nabokov at the Movies* where she explores filmic tropes and influences in Nabokov's writing. Wyllie explains how Humbert's consciousness in *Lolita* is 'saturated by film', deliberately adopting filmic styles and techniques to convey the landscape as they are driving past (137). The overabundance of these film-induced metaphors used to describe the environment begins to render it artificial and synthetic. Bourbon Street, Louisiana, is full of capering 'pickaninnies', tap-dancing for pennies (164). Arizona is 'obvious' with 'pueblo dwellings, aboriginal pictographs' and 'a dinosaur track in a desert canyon' (166). The Southern United States has 'movie ladies with sun-kissed shoulders' leaning over 'iron-trellis balconies and hand-worked stairs' in 'rich Technicolor' (165). This latter description is complete with the 'devoted Negress shaking her head on the upper landing'[2] (165). These filmic descriptions of natural landscapes and stock American figures are made artificial in Humbert's narration, implying stereotypes and flat character parodies. This suggests an exhaustion of stereotypes as cliché figures in Humbert's narration churned out by cinema. America's natural landscape is redefined in terms of movie signifiers that refashion its scenery into a marketable commodity. Humbert's movie-signified landscape transmutes the actual America into a cultural bricolage. These film influences are emphasized by the plethora of movies that Humbert and Lolita attend on the road in that one year. Cinematic influences reverberate through the entire novel.[3] giving credence to Humbert's own creative re-telling of America. This landscape manifests permissible dreamlike qualities that allow his own transgressions to slide through.

As Humbert and Dolores drive across a succession of twenty-seven states, his narrative language retains an outsider's wonder, lost in the depth of this strange country. His description of America combines a mixture of freshness and disease. Beautifully eroded clay and yucca blossoms are described as 'so pure, so waxy' but he also specifies as being 'lousy with creeping flies' (165). Natural beauty is marveled at in his list of mountains that are distant, near, and then more mountains which are unattainable 'bluish beauties'. The prehistoric or Wild West historical also creeps in amidst the present day description creating a strange mixture of the natural infused with the fantastic.

> Independence, Missouri, the starting point of the Old Oregon Trail; and Abilene, Kansas, the home of the Wild Bill Something Rodeo. Distant mountains. Near Mountains. More Mountains; bluish beauties never attainable, or ever turning into inhabited hill after hill; south-eastern ranges, altitudinal failures as alps go; heart and sky-piercing snow veined gray colossi of stone, relentless peaks appearing from nowhere at a turn of the highway; timbered enormities, with a system of neatly overlapping dark firs, interrupted in places by pale puffs of aspen; pink and lilac formations, Pharaonic, phallic, 'too prehistoric for words' (blasé Lo); buttes of black lava; early spring mountains with young elephant lanugo along their spines; end-of-the-summer mountain, all hunched up, their heavy Egyptian limbs folded under folds of tawny moth-eaten plush; oatmeal hills, flecked with green round oaks; a last rufous mountain with a rich rug of lucerne at its foot (165).

Humbert's descriptions translate the American landscape into a metaphysical environment inserted between filmic exaggeration and reality. He mentions Independence Missouri and Kansas, historically naming the cities as the starting point of the Old Oregon Trail. This situates the landscape in the heart of the Western frontier, with connotations of the Wild West, home of the 'Wild Bill Something Rodeo' (165). American landscape in the text and its historical specificities are blurred by the Hollywood mythologies with which it has been invested. The passage moves on dreamily, deliberately describing the mountain range in discordant proportions. The mountains are 'south-eastern', 'heart and sky-piercing'—giving an enchanted quality to the landscape. We move from blue and lilac formations to primeval descriptions of black lava and mountains creeping with 'young-elephant lanugo along their spines; as well as end-of-the-summer mountains described as folding their 'heavy Egyptian limbs' (165). These prehistoric signifiers coupled with Wild West filmic imagery, nostalgia history, and archly metaphorical prose; situate the American landscape in a particular uncanny interaction with Humbert, the European outsider. In *Lolita*, Humbert transforms the American landscape into something fantastical, repeatedly inventing and reinventing to create a permissible place to satiate his desires. Prehistoric mountains and pharonic imagery abound with the Wild West frontier, creating a time before moral laws and punitive legal concerns. The waxy yucca blossoms and sky-piercing mountains proliferate in highly metaphorical and beautifully arch prose, lulling one into forgetting the brutal application of his desires, daily enacted, lying behind this screen of language.

1. Marling also discusses gleaming stainware ads that were often compared to natural landscapes in America or how 'Tacy Lucy likes the stove with the glass picture window in the door of the oven' (4).

2. See Wyllie's discussion of descriptive passages in *Lolita* that evoke cinematic associations—Wyllie specifically discusses 'Southern Confederate style[s]' and allusions to *Gone with the Wind* (140).

3. The suburban atmosphere of Ramsdale in the first section of the text alludes to such popular films as *The Long Long Trailer* and *Tea for Two*. Films such as these aided in glorifying the cult of domesticity in the 1950s.

CHAPTER FOUR

THE UNDERWORLD: AMERICA AS MOVIE

As in Ramsdale suburbia, Humbert feels both attraction and repulsion towards America's greater social and geographical environment. Tawdry cultural landscape descriptions are also expressed by an unsettling outsider fetishizing the environment. On one hand, he disdainfully lists Dolores's attraction for vulgar signage:

> A great user of roadside facilities, my unfastidious Lo would be charmed by toilet signs — Guys-Gals, John-Jane, Jack-Jill and even Buck's-Doe's; ... (161)

And in the very next breath, he unwittingly commits the same offense by eruditely fetishizing the environment:

> [W]hile lost in an artist's dream, I would stare at the honest brightness of the gasoline paraphernalia against the splendid green of oaks, or at a distant hill scrambling out — scarred but still untamed — from the wilderness of agriculture that was trying to swallow it (161).

Humbert's lush, metaphorical narration of small town America — leaping from sprawling wilderness to luminescent gas stations — though fetishized, is vividly recounted. The American environment is cradled and coddled through Humbert's fetish, becoming nothing more than his personal artifice. Boyd aptly illustrates this relationship with Lolita when he writes: 'he appropriates her on his own terms, just as he will appropriate all of America to make a paradise for himself and a prison for his little girl' (229). Humbert's description of landscape grows progressively stranger as he attempts to equate the environment with a dreamscape or film world where his desires are slightly more permissible:

> [B]ut gradually the models of those elementary rusticities became stranger and stranger to the eye, the nearer I came to know them. Beyond the tilled plain, be-

yond the toy roofs, there would be a slow suffusion of inutile loveliness, a low sun in a platinum haze with a warm peeled-peach tinge pervading the upper edge of a two-dimensional, dove-gray cloud fusing with the distant amorous mist (161).

The metaphysical descriptions of landscape produce a dream world 'fusing with the distant amorous mist' (161). The 'warm peeled-peach tinge' bathes the description in muted colors giving a 'slow suffusion of inutile loveliness' to the airborne prose. The houses have 'toy roofs' and the platinum sun envelopes everything in beautiful colors; Humbert even including a 'two-dimensional' cloud to complete the enchanting image he has drawn for us. This romantic scene elevates his desires for America and by extension Dolores Haze, substantiating his foreign presence in the country and as her companion. Frosch comments that Humbert recognizes his ridiculous position of being a spokesman for values that nobody believes in anymore. His elegiac descriptions portray him as 'a romantic dreamer and enchanted poet' rather than a 'brutal scoundrel' and he self-deprecatingly acknowledges that his judges 'will regard his lyrical outbursts' as 'mummery' (89). Humbert's acknowledgement of his absurdity aids in his reinvention of a permissive America and a fanciful Lolita. His lyrical outbursts of rapture are a means of focusing the reader's mind on an essentially poetic and thereby uncontrollable sensibility: America and Lolita are so beautiful that he is morally dehabilitated. This aids 'his judges' in forgiving him for fetishizing American culture and, by extension, its available actualization, Dolores Haze.

Other passages however, frequently contrast with this type of language and instead of archly metaphorical prose, Humbert will counter with extensive lists of cultural artifacts found at destinations:

We passed and re-passed through the whole gamut of American roadside restaurants, from the lowly Eat with its deer head (dark trace of long tear at inner canthus), 'humorous' picture post cards of the posterior 'Kurort' type, impaled guest checks, life savers, sunglasses, adman visions of celestial sundaes, one half of a chocolate cake under glass, and several horribly experienced flies zigzagging over the sticky sugar-pour on the ignoble counter; (163).

Humbert's description becomes a mix of the archly literary when referring to the pastoral landscape and ironical, when wearily listing 'low' cultural artifacts. These descriptions also support his case as they substantiate his elevation of America and Lolita from their sordid vulgar reality.

Frosch pinpoints a central conflict in the text between 'Humbert's old-world, European manner' placed against America's brassiness or more specifically, 'his formal elegant style of speaking posed against Lolita's slang' (89). In Part Two of the novel, Humbert places the two language styles side by side, often directly following each other. In many cases, he hybridizes the language styles further, juxtaposing dreamy pastoral images with manmade cultural artifacts in the same sentence, creating such strange metaphorical imagery as 'tall trucks studded with colored lights, like dreadful giant Christmas trees,' and then a steady mountain range 'dun grading into blue, and blue into dream' and finally, in the same breath, a whirling desert consisting of 'dust, gray thorn bushes, and hideous bits of tissue paper mimicking pale flowers among the prickles of wind-tortured withered stalks all along the highway' (161-2). Tall trucks are transformed into trees and tissue paper turned into flowers. A Claude Lorrain landscape becomes a gas station and a mountain range, giving way to hideous tissue-paper mimicries of flowers. Cars transform and disappear into the heat, mountains are described in such euphoric language that they disappear into a dream and then into desert and suddenly, desert becomes highway. This not only demonstrates the interaction of both high culture (European influenced natural landscape) as well as low culture (gas station signs and rubbish), but manifests an uncanniness in vision; through the guise of wonder and parody in Humbert's cultural panopticon.

This filmic environment that Humbert invents transforms the American landscape into a reinvented and more permitting environment. To substantiate the permeating filmic influence, Humbert relates to us how during that one year, he and Lolita viewed 'one hundred and fifty or two hundred films, seeing many of the same newsreels half a dozen times, her favourite genres in order of 'musicals, underworlders, and westerners' (180). He meticulously describes reiterated themes and action sequences in American films that mimic in his own narrative:

> The underworld was a world apart: there, heroic newspapermen were tortured, telephone bills ran to billions, and, in a robust atmosphere of incompetent marksmanship, villains were chased through sewers and storehouses by pathologically fearless cops (I was to give them less exercise) (180).

Humbert conveys a criminal society sinister only in its outrageousness, a world manifesting great comedic potential. The pairing of his own misdemeanours with this outlandish underworld subtly dismisses his own ethical trespasses. Humbert parodies criminal film narrative, yet calculatingly identifies with it as well: 'I was to give them less exercise' (180). His actions associate with a fantastic reality that tempers and defamiliarizes his moral transgressions against Dolores Haze. In *Lolita*, 'heroic' marksmen are not tortured, only the debauched Quilty. A 'robust atmosphere of incompetent marksmanship' is present in the novel but it is not the fearless cops shooting, only the ridiculous Humbert. His last remark '(I was to give them less exercise)' is conspicuously in brackets, visibly pretending to be an afterthought in the passage. This clever move unequivocally aligns the unrealistic criminal/cop movie world with his defamiliarized reality. This theme is directly reiterated later in Humbert and Lolita's last scene together, Humbert leaving with the words: 'Then I pulled out my automatic' acting as a parody and direct reference to Western landscape mentioned here (297). Humbert depicts this suppositious narrative allowing it to proliferate on the surface of a veiled America. This filmic reinvention is made vivid with the mahogany landscape, the florid-faced, blue-eyed, roughriders:

> the prim pretty schoolteacher arriving in Roaring Gulch, the rearing horse, the spectacular stampede, the pistol thrust through the shivered window-pane, the stupendous fist fight, the crashing mountain of dusty old-fashioned furniture, the table used as a weapon, the timely somersault, the pinned hand still groping for the dropped bowie knife, the grunt, the sweet crash of fist against chin, the kick in the belly, the flying tackle; and immediately after a plethora of pain that would have hospitalized a Hercules (I should know by now), nothing to show but the rather becoming bruise on the bronzed cheek of the warmed-up hero embracing his gorgeous frontier bride (180).

Filmic images are conjured, contextualizing the Wild West and the lawless nature of the United States especially during its Frontier period. The Last Frontier imagery is telling as Humbert's recurring theme, used to comically disassociate his moral culpability from his actions. Such images as 'the stupendous fist fight' and 'the timely somersault' foreshadow his showdown with Quilty. However, Humbert is much more battered than a 'becoming bruise' as the end of his fight implies, and his 'gorgeous frontier bride' is seventeen, heavily pregnant with another man's child, soon to slip into death. The gap between cinema and reality is emphasized in this example, Humbert's American reinvention made inadequate by the imperfect glimmer of reality behind the cinematic screen. Direct comparisons are made between film and his own narrative, transforming the American landscape he experiences with fantastic cinematic qualities. He is still morally culpable; however, there is a gap between reality and cinema suggesting an America that escapes his observation and hermeneutic narrative. As Stark observes, 'Humbert usually attributes reality to his world and its center, Lolita; he merely *transmutes* them imaginatively' (101, ital mine). The number of readers that allow Humbert exemption from moral responsibility proves just how convincingly Humbert refashions America and Dolores.

CHAPTER FIVE

THE RESUSCITATION OF THE ROMANCE GENRE

In the last chapter, I discussed the reconstruction of American landscape through the appropriation of filmic imagery. The landscape and storyline become fantastic as Humbert increasingly introduces filmic styles and techniques. These cinematic influences serve not only as imagery sources but also as structural elements relating to genres in the text. *Lolita* mixes traditional with non-traditional filmic and literary genres such as romance, fantasy, the buddy story, along with 'low brow' literature forms such as the comic book and sentimental romances. Several critics have discussed *Lolita*'s extensive parody of genre, Boyd commenting that the text 'inverts the detective story pattern' (243), and Appel investigating the way such subgenres of fiction and film produce the novel's integrated literary dialogue (15). The introduction of comic book materials from Dolores Haze's reading matter of choice, and the general ransacking of comedic imagery in the text push the novel into the realms of pastiche. The cryptogrammatic chase of Quilty and Dolores in the second cross-country road trip deliberately mirrors and parodies the first journey taken by Humbert and Lolita. Humbert and Lolita's first road trip involves a mix of genres, alluding to the buddy journey, father/daughter bonding trip, as well as the romantic quest. These genres are formally alluded to in the first cross country road trip, but are twisted by the plot in *Lolita*. Humbert and Dolores are not 'buddies'; he illegally kidnaps her from camp and spirits her across several states in America. In one breath, Dolores will ask Humbert if they are lovers, and in the next, refer to him as her 'Dad' (120-1). As a couple, they are a perversion of the father/daughter relationship — Dolores often only mockingly referring to Humbert as 'Dad', 'let[ing] the word expand with ironic deliberation' (119). Such dialogue sequences parody the familial bond relationship in sentimental novels and film, making strange the formulaic sequence of a developing romance story. Humbert will burst into poetic flights of fancy describing his Lolita, yet also threaten

Dolores with the story that they are outlaws together; her actions will garner as much punitive retribution as his actions. Dolores is not Humbert's buddy or friend, but his isolation and the corruption of her mind and body give her no other choice but to accede to his re-imagination of her. Almost discovered debauching his daughter in the middle of a forest, Humbert grabs her, and as he puts it, 'with the quiet murmured order one gives a sweatstained distracted cringing trained animal even in the worst of plights…I made Lo get up, and we decorously walked, and then indecorously scuttled down to the car' (179). This scene among others perverts the idea of the buddy narrative, the traditional middle-American father and daughter relationship, as well as sabotaging Humbert's crafted re-imagining of America and Dolores Haze. Several levels of defamiliarization are occurring in the text, with Humbert firstly reinventing an America to permit his physical desires and Nabokov secondly, structurally undermining his protagonist using parody and linguistic subversion. Such insidious written comments as being 'faced with the distasteful task of recording a definite drop in Lolita's morals', demonstrate Nabokov's mockery and repulsion of his main narrator (194).

In discussing where to place the text genrewise, John Hollander and Thomas Frosch have interpreted *Lolita* as a resuscitation of the romance novel. *Lolita*, Frosch argues, is the ultimate un-possessable object, with Humbert creating a series of romantic structures that are doomed to failure (83). Frosch makes a valid point here, and although he does not develop its implications to any great length, this concept can be developed further if we think of Lolita as almost an invented conceit, not un-possessable because Humbert creates doomed romantic structures, but because Humbert re-imagines her. She is both girl and fabrication—this is how Humbert excuses himself as Lolita appears between her disclosed reality and his uncanny representation of her. Nabokov undermines Humbert's reinvention this way, revealing his canny and calculated motives, however disguised by his romantic idealization. The girl Lolita exists only through Humbert's re-imagining of her in his narrative. Humbert's love is the most convincing when he uses richly metaphorical prose to conjure a girl at odds with her character's own dialogue. This dialogue is also only present to us within Humbert's first-person narrative account of their relationship. At one moment Humbert can represent Lolita exclusively through his idealizing lens:

> She was my Lolita again—in fact, more of my Lolita than ever. I let my hand rest on her warm auburn head and took her bag. She was all rose and honey, dressed in her brightest gingham, with a pattern of little red apples, and her arms and legs were of a deep golden brown, with scratches like tiny dotted lines of coagulated rubies, and the ribbed cuffs of her white socks were turned down at the remembered level, and because of her childish gait, or because I had memorized her as always wearing heelless shoes, her saddle oxfords looked somehow too large and too high-heeled for her (118).

And at another moment reveal a completely different girl almost unequal in vulgarity:

> Some twenty miles earlier I had happened to tell her that the day school she would attend at Beardsley was a rather high-class, non-coeducational one, with no modern nonsense, whereupon Lo treated me to one of those furious harangues of hers where entreaty and insult, self-assertion and double talk, vicious vulgarity and childish despair, were interwoven in an exasperating semblance of logic which prompted a semblance of explanation from me. Enmeshed in her wild words (swell chance...I'd be a sap if I took your opinion seriously ...Stinker...You can't boss me...I despise you....and so forth), I drove through the slumbering town at a fifty-mile-per-hour pace in continuance of my smooth highway swoosh, and a twosome of patrolmen put their spotlight on the car, and told me to pull over (181).

These gaping irregularities portraying the same character in the text emphasize a wide contrast between the 'real' Dolores Haze and Humbert's re-invention of her. We have considerable differences between a 'golden brown' nymphet and the furious spitting child who is allowed to articulate her adolescent despair only in brackets—'(Stinker...You can't boss me...)'. These discrepancies within the narrative reiterate Humbert's lack of mastery in the text and demonstrate his imperfect transformation of Lolita and America. Lolita is the unattainable object, not because of the romantic structures and narrative twists of the book, but because she is a partially re-invented girl. Wood endorses this idea in his chapter 'The Language of Lolita':

> The actual Lolita is the person we see Humbert can't see, or can see only spasmodically. In this sense she is a product of reading, not because the reader makes her one or because she is just 'there' in the words, but because she is what a reading finds, and I would say needs to find in order to see the range of what the book can do. She needs to be 'there', that is, and she needs to be found (117).

Boyd also endorses this view, stating that Nabokov creates a Lolita far rounder and richer than the flat image described by Humbert. He refutes Stella Estes letter to Nabokov who writes, 'Lolita is a charming brat lifted from an ordinary existence only by the special brand of love bestowed upon her' (236, qtd. in Boyd). Humbert does not lose her, as Frosch implies, because she is the unobtainable prize in an aforeconcluded romance novel, but because the real Dolores Haze exists very slimly in the text. Humbert rarely allows her a voice in the novel, and if she does speak, it is only through the intervention of his narrative. The meager times that her voice is heard answering Humbert in quick repartee demonstrate that her sharp and witty mind remains unutilized, just as her sobbings in the night are only heard in the distance, placed as an afterthought to Humbert's elegiac prose. Imprinted on the surface of her existence is another more metaphorically enchanting Lolita that exists only in Humbert's narrative. Stark substantiates this by noting that Lolita's more magical qualities exist only in Humbert's imagination (82). In comparing *Lolita* to Nabokov's other fanciful love story *Ada*, Stark makes the point that Humbert transforms a girl who should be unattractive to him and other adult males into an 'irresistible object', therefore 'replacing reality more completely than anyone in *Ada* does' (98). One must emphasize that Lolita is definitely a *re-invention* and not an *invention* as the real Dolores Haze does exist, but only through visible lapses in the narrative. Nabokov allows her a voice through dialogue, demonstrating that another girl exists behind Humbert's characterization. Stark comments that Humbert is 'capable of distinguishing between the two', as he frequently records the existence of Dolores and Lolita in the novel, juxtaposing passages of her vulgarity with his fanciful re-imagination of her qualities (70). Humbert's deliberate and *knowing* re-imagination of her qualities implicates his moral and ethical trespasses. Humbert defamiliarizes her to allow himself moral culpability, but the very nature of his re-imagination forbids him any chance of possessing her. Smith writes of Dolores Haze being 'a garden, a palace and twilight' remaining forever closed to Humbert's re-invention—a misstep in dialogue, a secret knowing look, an uncertain metaphor that does not allow complete moral reprehensibility—such passages are vivid in Dolores' troubled silences, the great division between her voice and his trochaic description of her, as well as in their final encounter (89).

In 'Parody and Authenticity in *Lolita*', Frosch outlines a series of typical romance structures, demonstrating that each situation in *Lolita* is a 'version of the quest, or hunt, and each one an embodiment of a specific type of suspense or anxiety' (83). Frosch details specific plot developments that are integral to his argument regarding the essentially romantic structuring of the text. The first structure revolves around the introduction and pursuit of Lolita and the anxiety of overstepping physical sexual boundaries. Once the two are lovers, there is a new anxiety about Humbert's possession being taken away. This anxiety is directed against other boys and men, and ultimately, the unknown stranger who pursues them. Lastly, Frosch details Humbert's altercations with Quilty and how these involvements explicitly fall into the double story and revenge plot (83). Though Frosch is convincing in his explicit layout of romantic structures in *Lolita*, he neglects to mention that Nabokov parodies these layouts almost step by step. Frosch conscientiously outlines the Hum/Lo road trip as parodic of romantic structure, what he neglects to examine is the second road trip involving Quilty that is a parody of the first parody, more closely resembling pastiche.

The second cross-country journey with Humbert chasing Quilty and Dolores serves to parody and defamiliarize the structures chosen in the first cross-country road trip. There is an uncanny sensation of genre being inverted: Humbert replaying his roadtrip and becoming his own ghostly double by following Quilty and Lolita. The second journey uses different genres—mystery, detective story, and cartoon comic—to parody the genres established in the first journey—romantic quest, buddy and father/daughter familial bonding. In the second cross-country trip, the father/daughter bonding is turned on its head with the father now chasing his 'daughter' with her lover, except that Humbert is a meager representation of a father and Quilty is his age with an uncanny resemblance to him. This mystery chase is inflated to bumbling proportions, Humbert thinking every register name a mocking clue, acting as the rescuer when he was the kidnapper only a few chapters before. Nabokov parodies these genres, further defamiliarizing them by using other genres to reverse them yet again into comic strangeness. This second chase develops the parody in the novel as it echoes the first chase, which is a parody of the detective genre itself. This idea of blank parody, or the parodying of nothingness can be ascribed to Frederic Jameson's theory of 'pastiche' in which the text contains nothing but 'blank parody' or 'like parody, the imitation of a peculiar or unique, idiosyncratic style, the wearing of a linguistic mask, speech in a dead language' (*Postmodernism*, 17). Working from this concept, we can see that the second chase scene robs Humbert and Dolores's journey of intense significance; he backtracks across the same states that the first road trip covered in such a dreamy and longing manner. The first road trip has fantastic filmic imagery of such epic proportions that we realize Humbert's longing for Dolores is mirrored in the cinematic and dreamy landscape. This transforms Dolores into Lolita, his ideal lover, and keeps Humbert as the handsome foreign movie star. The second journey across America robs the first journey's iridescent qualities, becoming a wild and comical goose chase. The ridiculous nature of the return trip acts to undermine qualities conveyed in the first trip. This second trip also encompasses several suspect genres such as low brow detective fiction and the comic book genre, thus devaluing entrenched ideals and emotions already declared by Humbert in the first trip. The landscape, earlier conveyed in lush and dreamy prose, is now revisited and dismissed in favor of the manic, desperate chase. The first trip has language moving across the landscape in an exaggerated romance style, depicting 'heavenly-hued blossoms that I would fain call larkspur crowded all along a purly mountain brook' (178). The second trip differs in that Humbert is obsessed only with Quilty's paper trail, leaving scant description of his surroundings. There is little scenic description; the first trip which describes America in such caressing, languorous terms — 'that mountain country…rolling down an almost imperceptible grade' has retracted into the finicky study of motel registers and pedantic literary, as well as self-referential allusions.

Parody and pastiche also collaborate with repetition as a structural technique in *Lolita*. Quilty's reappearance everywhere demonstrates this; he is a ghostly presence in Ramsdale, precedes Lolita and Humbert as a guest at the Enchanted Hunters Hotel, and turns up in Beardsley directing the play that Lolita stars in. Lolita's camp is even nicknamed 'Camp Q'. It is also an uncanny coincidence that the hotel where Lolita and Humbert first consummate their relationship holds the same name as Quilty's play involving virgin sacrifice as subject matter in Beardsley (Boyd, 246). Other examples of pattern genre inversion include Humbert's attempt to seduce Lolita, and Lolita's turning around and seducing him. Likewise, when Humbert plans to murder Charlotte but is unable to bring the plan into action, "McFate" runs her over with a fortuitous accident. The overturning of Humbert's carefully laid plans by an omniscient force juxtaposes the careful setup and the unexpected inversion of filmic and literary genres. Nabokov structurally parodies these romantic tropes and genres to the point of pastiche, thus further emphasizing alienation and strangeness in the text.

CHAPTER SIX

DEFAMILIARIZATION AND LANGUAGE

'For all the world, like the cheapest of cheap cuties'
-Humbert in *Lolita*

Humbert's highly artificial language is obliged to co-exist with his relentless registration of vernacular details and popular forms of American life. These are only two of several different kinds of language variations dispersed throughout *Lolita*. Subversive language forms play an integral part in the novel's defamiliarization of America. Different forms of American-English—slang, highly elaborate figures (especially metaphor), parody, the faux refinement of suburban American, magazine speak, advertising jargon, unconscious imitation of cinematic script—all contribute to the linguistic creation of the American cultural landscape of the fifties. These different forms of American language insert disjunctures into Humbert's narration. Humbert himself pays close attention to the different forms of American-English, sometimes parodying juvenile slang, sometimes archly placing it in quotation marks within his highly metaphorical prose, and other times, slyly slipping it into his dialogue, ingratiating himself with Charlotte or Dolores Haze. Humbert's exacting scrutiny of the rigidly conventional patterns of American life and speech discloses rich opportunities for his turning, by a twist of language, what seems normal to his deviant purposes. He makes the innocent American world strange by his linguistic deviance and discovers its counter-image behind the cheerful surface.

Although *Lolita* is a first person narrative, we hear not only Humbert's voice but also faint echoes of the other characters' voices in the text. Humbert the narrator transcribes and comments on a cross-section of American cultural and geographical landscapes. He deliberately alters American linguistic landscape so we need to filter that record through his irony and allow for his imperfect and disdainful foreign ear. Humbert carries a mini America with him in the person of Lolita who is both a metonymy for American popular culture and an avenue into its speech and norms. Though *Lolita* is a confessional narrative told in the first person, the interaction between numerous different voices draws attention to other narratives besides Humbert's. American English in *Lolita* cannot be regarded as monolithic, communicating and interacting in a single voice. In fact, as Bakhtin has famously demonstrated, most languages often produce a heightened tension between the drive towards a unitary monolithic voice, and a heteroglossic multitude of voices (270). This unitary language is made up of a system of linguistic norms that is in constant opposing tension with 'heteroglossia' or the multitude of voices that deviate from the unitary voice. In *Lolita*, heteroglossia is contained within the seemingly autocratic voice of the narrator as quotation and disdainful reference as well as in the other voices insinuated in the narrative.

Heteroglossia refers to a number of different voices that interact in discordant as well as accordant harmony within the text. In *Lolita*, Humbert's dominant first person narration attempts to keep the heteroglossic voices silent. This is demonstrated by his quickness to speak for Lolita, as well as his ready anticipation of Charlotte's thoughts and feelings. Brian McHale notes that modernist texts often 'integrate the multiple worlds of discourse into a single ontological plane', creating something akin to a 'unified projected world' (*Postmodernist Fiction*, 166). Humbert strives for this unification in his confessional narrative. He is under pressure to have his tale believed, keeping the other voices under control, and subsequently allowing his necessary inventions to replace those glimmering underneath. Authorial hegemony is impossible, however, and McHale acknowledges that although Humbert strives towards unification, 'heteroglossia is not easily kept under control' and a 'centrifugal counterpressure' is exerted on the text (*Postmodernist* 166). Heteroglossia includes not only various language dialects and foreign influences, but also specific language styles, social dialects, and cultural as well as sociological placements in the language. In *Lolita*, until Dolly is changed into a nymphet and Dolores into Lolita[1] we have American slang, advertising rhetoric, high metaphor and lists of fetishized artifacts. Humbert imagines his twelve-year-old subject as his daughter, lover and aging mistress, inventing her title in turn as 'Annabel', 'Carmen', and even as a 'young slave'. This reinvention of personality through the bestowment of names contributes to the idea of language as actively engaging in a dialogue, a dialogue that becomes explicit in the mingling of voices characteristic of novelistic discourse. This dialogic mingling aids in making Humbert's verbal world strange. Although language is conventionally represented in a monolithic manner with a unitary voice, the presence of disharmonic voices engaging in dialogue indicates that there is disharmony that sounds within the harmony. Humbert's attempts to master control and maintain an authoritative voice in the narrative is often overridden by the heteroglossia in the text. Bakhtin claims that these unifying and collapsing forces act in a constant tension, which is evoked every time the language is spoken. In this way, the 'concrete utterance of a speaking subject' is the very space 'centrifugal as well as centripetal forces' simultaneously oppose each other (272).

This heteroglossic multitude of voices occurs in Lolita via a traditional storytelling tactic that Bakhtin refers to as character objectification. Bakhtin explains that 'the more objectified a character, the more sharply his speech physiognomy stands out' (183). Social and class dialects, language styles, literary allusions and slang all contribute to revealing the characters. In *Lolita*, Humbert's arch metaphorical language interacts with Dolores' jazzy slang. Humbert's trochaic descriptions are used to describe an advertising-jingle landscape, Cozy Comforts and Sleepy Nite Inns. Charlotte Haze's character is revealed as her jangle is repeatedly mocked by Humbert's ironic literary language:

> With the zest of a banal young bride, she started to 'glorify the home' (81).
>
> She rearranged the furniture—and was pleased when she found, in a household treatise, that 'it is permissible to separate a pair of sofa commodes and their companion lamps' (82).
>
> 'That is not the point', said the logical doomed dear (86).

Humbert's contempt in expressing Charlotte's attitudes and voice include the satirizing of American magazine lingo. Most of Charlotte's voice is relayed in quotation marks ('glorify the home' and 'companion lamps') signifying her direct citations from contemporary magazines or newspapers. Since Charlotte's voice directly engages in constant dialogue with American advertising culture, her identity becomes seamlessly combined with commercialism. When Humbert mocks Charlotte, he is not only parodying Charlotte's voice, but also the echo of American contemporary culture. This is further emphasized by his description and character study of Dolores Haze:

> She believed, with a kind of celestial trust, any advertisement or advice that appeared in *Movie Love* or *Screen Land*—Starasil Starves Pimples, or 'You better watch out if you're wearing your shirttails outside your jeans, gals, because Jill says you shouldn't.' If a roadside sign said: VISIT OUR GIFT SHOP—we *had* to visit it, *had* to buy its Indian curios, dolls, copper jewelry, cactus candy. The words 'novelties and souvenirs' simply entranced her by their trochaic lilt... She it was to whom ads were dedicated: the ideal consumer, the subject and object of every foul poster (156).

Dolores is engaged, like her mother, in an active dialogue with the culture of advertising. Her actions and attitudes are heavily influenced by this commercial discourse. Humbert parodies the language of both Dolores and her mother, engaging in a subversive dialogue and narrative percolating underneath the surface conversations. Bakhtin describes parody as language that actually exceeds the limits of linguistics and becomes *metalinguistic* (185, my itals). In terms of dialogue and discourse, Bakhtin describes parody as having twofold direction: it is directed at both the object of the speaker (as in regular discourse) and also 'to

ward someone else's speech' (185). Thus, Humbert's parody of Lolita's speech constitutes a dialogue in its own terms, separate from Lolita's dialogue with advertising culture.

A good example of the heteroglossic voices in the text is where Humbert is caught in his false role as Charlotte's loving husband:

> My hand still on the doorknob, I repeated my hearty cry. Her writing hand stopped. She sat still for a moment; then she slowly turned in her chair and rested her elbow on its curved back. Her face, disfigured by her emotion, was not a pretty sight as she stared at my legs and said:
> 'The Haze woman, the big bitch, the old cat, the obnoxious mamma, the—the old stupid Haze is no longer your dupe. She has—she has...' (101).

It is telling that the instant of Humbert's new-found familiarity with the Ramsdale home coincides with Charlotte's discovery of his imposture. Humbert is forbidden to feel comfortable in his American setting for long and Nabokov is careful to keep him isolated as an interloper. Charlotte's discovery of Humbert's fraudulent role causes his brief familiarity with American suburbia to instantly transform his world into a hostile and alien setting. It is also significant that the uncovering of Humbert's false role causes Charlotte to mimic his insulting words back at him: 'The big bitch, the old cat, the obnoxious mama, the old stupid Haze' are vulgar insults that have not been part of Humbert's linguistic repertoire before. Previously, Humbert has always used the most ironical of comments when discussing Charlotte, describing her as 'my poor wife', or 'the poor woman', or even more strongly: 'like a musician who may be an odious vulgarian in ordinary life' (81, 88). Humbert's baroque internal monologue is broken up as vulgar blasphemies erupt in this part of the narrative. His complete mastery over the text lapses, allowing other voices to appear in the narrative. The insults that Charlotte finds in Humbert's journal are his hidden linguistic imprint, only revealed through the parodic repetition of another discourse slipping beyond his control. Humbert remains the narrator, but the other characters are significantly able to engage in dialogue beyond his supervision.

Humbert's arch metaphorical style engages with his vulgar insulting style (kept hidden in his journal), and is revealed only through Charlotte's hysterical patter. This exposure through another character's parody is significant because it actively demonstrates a subversive linguistic communication which is separate from the monolithic narrative. Parody, as Bakhtin and Hutcheon have argued, is a covert method used to engage in alternate dialogues in a text.[2] Hutcheon defines it as a type of communication that 'takes the form of self-conscious, self-contradictory, self-undermining statement' (*Politics*, 1). Parody as a heteroglossic voice therefore aids in defamiliarizing by disrupting the master narrative.

Humbert's first person narrative becomes untrustworthy because other characters manage to covertly reveal aspects of his personality that he attempts to hide. Parody is often politically double coded, meaning that 'it both legitimizes and subverts that which it parodies' (Hutcheon, 101). This covert language also reiterates Humbert's strangeness and the fact that he remains an outsider who cannot be easily apprised or known in the text. The reader is challenged and in unfamiliar territory due to feeling sympathy towards Humbert, yet uncomfortably realizes that the narrator is inconsistent in his adopted role. Thus, Humbert's conversations with Charlotte and Dolores are never private; they never involve one voice interacting with another individual voice. The multiple instances of magazine language, advertising jingles, print and written glossies, and movie and television induced voices invade the consciousness of every character in the novel, and Humbert endlessly parodies and comments on this fact, so that he too is invaded:

> The sincerity and artlessness with which she discussed what she called her 'love-life', from first necking to connubial catch-as-catch-can, were, ethically, in striking contrast with my glib compositions, but technically the two sets were congeneric since both were affected by the same stuff (soap operas, psychoanalysis, and cheap novelettes) upon which I drew for my characters and she for her mode of expression (84).

Humbert realizes here that both he and Charlotte draw from the same plethora of cultural voices to construct their mutual relationship. Charlotte unconsciously imitates American penny romances to project her feelings of love. Humbert consciously draws from the same material, but uses it to manipulate her. Dana Brand's 'The Interaction of Aestheticism' suggests that Humbert's seizure of Charlotte's commercial colloquialisms to ironically mock her drains advertising of its coercive power (15). Exploring this argument further, one can further conclude that Humbert not only subverts, but also uses suburban-genteel language to invent a new Charlotte, gaining exemption from moral responsibility. In *Lolita,* we are only acquainted with the ridiculous Charlotte who is mocked through Humbert's voice. She is portrayed as a lovesick widow, blinded by Humbert's handsomeness to his true intentions:

> I simply can't tell you how gentle, how touching my poor wife was. At breakfast, in the depressingly bright kitchen, with its chrome glitter and Hardware and Co. Calendar and cute breakfast nook (simulating that Coffee Shoppe where in their college days Charlotte and Humbert used to coo together), she would sit, robed in red, her elbow on the plastic-topped table, her cheek propped on her fist, and stare at me with intolerable tenderness as I consumed my ham and eggs (81).

Humbert anticipates Charlotte's reactions and manipulates her thought processes to suit his reinvention of her character. He hyperbolizes to such an extent that he accuses her of building a 'breakfast nook' to simulate their imaginary college days. This is unreliable narration at its most cunning.[3] Humbert portrays a delusionary Charlotte, so blinded by love as to create a shared past with her foreign lodger. What Humbert insidiously achieves with this memory is to emphasize his and Charlotte's *shared* college days, implying his American belonging. This is an invented fiction, but Humbert cagily makes it Charlotte's invention, and something he conveniently appropriates. This furthers his pretense of being an insider, more comfortably slipping into his role as an American husband and father sipping coffee in suburbia. Thus, Humbert trickily achieves the double role of evaluating American culture as an outsider, yet reinventing Americans to aid in forging his role as an insider. Brand's analysis that sign-systems in *Lolita* are 'drained of their immanence' by Humbert is a useful one, but Humbert actually takes this process one step further in appropriating the American language to suit his morally depraved purposes.

Humbert's attempts at reinvention are reinforced during his last encounter with Lolita many years later. Earlier in this chapter, we discussed the unconvincing nature of Humbert's moral transformation, insisting that he loved the pregnant, polluted Dolly and not the nymphet Lolita all along. For us as readers, believing in this fiction is the equivalent of allowing Humbert to exorcise his demons and redeem himself. Wood effectively states that 'what he [Humbert] wants to evoke and renounce in his last meeting with Lolita is the guilt not of having slept with her but of having treated her as a sample or a treasure, a hoarded specimen of nymphetry, rather than a person' (138). This reinforces Humbert's systematic reinvention and defamiliarization of Dolores Haze throughout the narrative. Humbert's last painful meeting with Dolly Schiller has seduced many critics: Lance Olsen referring to it as redemption in 'passionate, stunning and painfully candid prose' (57) and Lionel Trilling acknowledging that he felt his moral rectitude and boundaries challenged (13). Olsen is convinced into romancing truths for Humbert, stating that '[h]e finds her even more extraordinary now than then, complexly textured and fully alive, because she is free from his brutal solipsism' (57). When Humbert asks her to run away with him, she refuses, stating that she would sooner go back to Quilty:

> 'I'll die if you touch me', I said. 'You are sure you are not coming with me? Is there no hope of your coming? Tell me only this.'
> 'No', she said. 'No, honey, no.'
> She had never called me honey before.
> 'No', she said, 'it is quite out of the question. I would sooner go back to Cue. I mean—'
> She groped for words. I supplied them mentally ('*He* broke my heart. *You* merely broke my life') (296).

Crucially, Humbert still has to supply the words for Dolores; she doesn't actually speak them, he appropriates her language. Olsen brushes this mimicry off as something that '[he] knows she means', but this is unconvincing; Dolly should supply her own words at this climatic moment, not submit to our unreliable narrator. When asked details about her sordid affair with Quilty, she has problems relating it to Humbert, 'groping' at language, unable to speak, and finally reduced to gesturing: 'and for lack of words spread the five fingers of her angularly up-and-down-moving hand' (293). Humbert's reinvention of the girl defamiliarizes the plot up to his very last meeting and thus blinds even his most alert readers. His climactic redemption fools us, supplying both voices in the text and forbidding Dolores Haze to speak. The only slips we get are images: her changed appearance, a certain way she looks, reading between the silences and the words left glimmering and unsaid. Thus we see that the linguistic flotsam and heteroglossic jetsam are not the only defamiliarizing element; there is also Humbert, but Humbert parodying his own narrative and reinventing the character's voices.

Humbert's ambivalent fascination with American speech patterns parallels that of his creator. Nabokov himself has provided a useful word from his native Russian for describing the particular quality of American life transcribed into language, which seems to fascinate his pedophilic protagonist. In Nabokov's book on Gogol, he uses the Russian word 'poshlost', meaning something false and artificial, tawdrily overdone, but cunningly changes it to 'Posh lust', ushering in a variety of linguistic and metaphorical connotations that change along with the vowel from 'o' to 'u'. As he explains this linguistic alteration, the phrase can be used to describe:

> not only the obviously trashy but mainly the falsely important, the falsely beautiful, the falsely clever, the falsely attractive. To apply the deadly label of poshlism to something is not only an aesthetic judgment but also a moral indictment. The genuine, the guileless, the good is never poshlust. It is possible to maintain that a simple, uncivilized man is seldom if ever a poshlust since poshlism presupposes the veneer of civilization. A peasant has to become a townsman in order to become vulgar. A painted necktie has to hide the honest Adam's apple in order to produce poshlism (*Lectures on Russian*, 310).

What Nabokov explores in *Lolita* is whether America is Poshlust. The evidence of Poshlism includes the trashy, glittering and foolish cultural artifacts that embody America and make such a country repellent to the European Humbert's civilized palate. In *Lolita*, Humbert defamiliarizes America by sardonically reflecting on its low culture and reinventing characters to excuse his moral laxness in the way he treats them. *Poshlust* is significant as an indication of trashy taste, but often in disguise as as something great and beautiful. This is epitomized in what Boyd refers to as Humbert casting his 'outsider's ironic eye over glad ads and *Screen Spleen,* teenage America, housewives' America, the tidy turf of suburban lawns and the loud signs of a thousand quiet Main Streets' (Boyd, 228). A telling example of this mocking cynicism occurs near to the end of the text when

Humbert is cleaning out the much traveled car. Lolita having already disappeared, her only traces found underneath the car seat:

> One day I removed from the car and destroyed an accumulation of teen-magazines. You know the sort. Stone age at heart; up to date, or at least Mycenaean, as to hygiene. A handsome, very ripe actress with huge lashes and a pulpy red underlip, endorsing a shampoo. Ads and fads…. Invite Romance by wearing the Exciting New Tummy Flattener. Trims tums, nips hips. Tristam in Movielove. Yessir! The Joe-Roe marital enigma is making yaps flap. Glamorize yourself quickly and inexpensively. Comics. Bad girl dark hair fat father cigar; good girl red hair handsome daddums clipped mustache. Or that repulsive strip with the big gagoon and his wife, a kiddoid gnomide (270).

This passage is a key example of the lists-upon-lists of contemporary American culture that Humbert remarks upon—sometimes contemptuously, sometimes fetishizing—as an extension of Lolita, but never allowing to escape his attention. If one were to compile all these lists as the sum total description of America, the fundamentally informing presence of *Poshlust* could not be denied. However, there is inkling that Humbert misses something throughout the novel in his fetishizing of Dolores and America in trashy dialogue consisting of such gems as 'Trims tums' and 'nips hips'. *Poshlust* artifacts are present, but this American tale refuses to be thoroughly mocked, escapes complete parody, and manages to be aesthetically redeemed in the end. Stark explicitly links these ideas by pointing out that Nabokov 'transmutes the tawdry setting, like the nymphetomania, into art, just as Humbert's imagination transmutes Lolita into a glorious creature' (76). Humbert's confessional tale does not really work; he cannot fully control the linguistic play of the characters even though this text is a first person narration. A different America from the one that he describes flickers underneath. Characters covertly express their true desires by means of parody, sudden slips of recognition in the narrative, and plot elements that Humbert misunderstands or only realizes in retrospect. Overt and covert language interactions are all present in the text and escape his monolithic narrative and complete defamiliarization.

Notes

1. This linguistic defamiliarization process is emphasized further in the way that he even creates a term, 'nymphet,' which emphasizes his re-invention of her into a signifier and no longer a real girl.

2. Please refer to M.M. Bakhtin's book on *Discourse in Dostoevsky* and Hutcheon's book *The Politics of Postmodernism*.

3. For more on for more on Humbert as an unreliable narrator, refer to *Lolita: a Janus Text* by Lance Olsen 49-51).

SECTION TWO

THE CRYING OF LOT 49

'A metaphysical thriller in the form of a pornographic comic strip'

— *Time Magazine* (6 May, 1966)

CHAPTER SEVEN

THE INSIDE OUTSIDER: DEFAMILIARIZATION AND THE NARRATOR

At the close of Scott Fitzgerald's *The Great Gatsby*, the pilgrim fathers stare at a world 'commensurate to man's capacity for wonder' (171). It is a brief moment of aesthetic contemplation before desire meets opportunity and the destructive energy of greed is unleashed. But in that moment before imaginative grasp is translated into tawdry reality something redemptive is glimpsed, sufficient to give Gatsby's pursuit of the fallen Daisy a sense of romantic readiness that the flawed love object cannot wholly dispel. The barest trace of that redemptive moment still survives in Humbert's sordid love for his nymphet. Without his sexual purpose the love he claims to be driven by would be permissible, perhaps even noble; without his belief in beauty, the wrong he does to Lolita would be too nakedly pornographic a story to bear. Pynchon's Oedipa Maas inhabits an America of foundered dreams, wrecked Plymouths and paranoid enthusiasms. The old moment of contemplation, and with it, the sense of possibility, has dissipated. Yet Oedipa too projects longing, as well as disgust and disappointment onto her world. Her lyrical moments, however caught up in the proliferating craziness of contemporary America, pull the reader back so that America in all its fallenness is viewed from a distance, made strange not only by itself but also by just the hint of transcendence.

The tale of *Lolita* is of a conventional 1950s society that has created a seamless representation of itself as progressive and bountiful—everywhere ice cold drinks, department stores, adobe units, country motels—and hence unassailable normality. The only unmistakable weirdness is introduced by our panoptic narrator who transforms the overproduced artifacts of normalcy into a strangeness that is both corrupting and seductive. Humbert is uninterested in the openly deviant cultural forces in post-war America including writers such as

Jack Kerouac and Allen Ginsberg who were already shaping America's new counterculture. In *The Crying of Lot 49*, this alternative culture that Humbert fails to observe in *Lolita* dominates, becoming the primary discourse. *Lot 49* is America made crazier, but the craziness has been domesticated, embedded in the normal, made almost familiar.

Humbert's interest lies in the middle-ground of American culture. Where he is interested in the deviance found just below the bland surface of the normal, in Pynchon's *Lot 49*, the underground has proliferated and taken over. The paradigm shift between the 1950s and the 1960s in America is reflected in the two novels as a kind of continuous historical allegory. Read as a linear narrative, *Lolita* and *Lot 49* describe a transformation in cultural values: from the Betty Crocker matching furniture regiment of the fifties, to the hippie Californian counter-culture of the sixties. Pynchon acknowledges Oedipa's in-betweeness in *Lot 49*, claiming that she was unsuitable perhaps for Berkeley sixties 'marches and sit-ins' but useful in 'pursuing strange words in Jacobean texts' making her a 'rare creature indeed' (76). Pynchon's comment suggests Oedipa's outdated status. Her combination of specialized academic training and lack of revolutionary vigor was a defunct combination in the rebelliously charged environment of the 60s. As Frederic Jameson notes, 'the 60s had to happen the way it did', explaining that 'its opportunities and failures were inextricably intertwined, marked by the objective constraints and openings of a determinate historical situation...' (*Periodising*, 125). During this period, changes included everything from historical and philosophical trends, to a shift in which the alternative cultures of the fifties—drugs and rock and roll—became the primary discourse. Suburban housewife Oedipa Maas represents the go-between of these two decades, tenuously linking the conformist fifties with the turbulent sixties. Oedipa acts as the single thread of normalcy leading us between these two decades, her out-of-placeness becoming abundantly clear in San Narciso. She significantly moves from a domestic role in Kinneret to being an adulterous swinger in San Narciso, only few hundred miles away. Petillon responds to this new climate by referring to *Lot 49* as 'slightly off-key, the mood of an "awkward" transition between two epochs, a transitional period' (129).

Nabokov cunningly plays with the idea of authorial intention in *Lolita*, addressing the reader, drawing them into the moral obliquities of the text, and teasing them with a sense of design behind the words. In *Lot 49*, Pynchon also involves his reader in the process of paranoid 'reading' of a constructed world by way of his main character, Oedipa Maas. Throughout the novel, Oedipa deciphers her world through subjective interpretations of an elusive and multi-layered reality. She is the central and governing interpreter of events in *Lot 49*, a remnant of a disappearing order of 'normality'. However, as she adventures into a new cultural order she finds her means of making sense increasingly destabilized. Oedipa's Kinneret housewife role ill-prepares her for the extravagant craziness of San Narciso, which confers on her the quality of the naïf so that she views events as an awestruck, curious and unsettled outsider. As in *Lolita*, textual reality is skewed by the protagonist's overly subjective interpretation of events. In Nabokov's text, Humbert appropriates genuine cultural artifacts, using them to reinvent a cinematic and uncanny America. In *The Crying of Lot 49*, cultural artifacts are also appropriated, made strange, and given a wholly fresh and newly interpretative reading—here by an American housewife rather than an urbane pedophile.

Viewing *Lolita* and *Lot 49* as a continuous American narrative discloses cultural pattern shifts, tracing a revolutionary change from the fifties to the sixties. Suburban home life is no longer subversively abnormal as in *Lolita*, but has been radically disrupted in *Lot 49*. The move into the 1960s finds American identity so synonymous with mass media and film that all characters in *Lot 49* view themselves through a type of filmic reality. Description of household items and gleaming whiteware are replaced by special purpose bond issue districts, shopping nuclei, and freeways (12). *Lot 49* is localized within a single city and the different environments that Oedipa explores are tellingly contained within the space of a small metropolis. This contrasts to Humbert's cross-country tour in *Lolita* where he keenly observes America across a wide expanse of physical and social environments. Instead of covering varying American settings and cultural phenomena, *Lot 49* is set in San Narciso where a realm of extraordinary events is crammed claustrophobically into a single environment. Where Nabokov tackles the general American landscape, Pynchon uses San Narciso as a specific metaphor for America in its entirety.

The name Oedipa invokes that solver of riddles—Oedipus, who was destined to follow a logical chain of clues towards a binary conclusion. Oedipa's name alludes directly to her Greek predecessor as *Lot 49*'s plot revolves around her attempts to piece together the secret conspiracy of an underground postal system into a larger meaning. Oedipa (as reader) questions the master narrative of the main post system; *The Courier's Tragedy*: Invarity's corporations—searching for a counter-culture narrative that might provide a more adequate explanation. However, there is a rhetorical element to her inquiries as she senses that no satisfactory answers are possible. This gives Oedipa elements of a nostalgic filter: she is earnestly searching for meaning in a world where meanings have spun out of control. Tony Tanner emphasizes the nature of this desperate search, referring to *Lot 49* as an Augustinian novel, based on the tradition of searching for divine truth that will be satisfactorily resolved in the text's conclusion (156). Tanner illustrates Pynchon's fictional worlds as complex versions of Augustinian novels with Manichean characters who are fatally attracted to self-destruction (155).[1] Reading *Lot 49* through this lens, Tanner suggests that the novel cannot decide whether to successfully parody an Augustinian novel or spiral destructively towards a Manichaean text. Tanner suggests that the alternative plot which Oedipa uncovers encompasses both 'that dream of annihilation' and 'those hopes for transcendence' that have been familiar in American thought since Emerson (179). Oedipa's binary notions of achievement and discovery are in keeping with the Augustinian search for answers with a clear goal resolvable at the end of the quest. However, Augustinian notions of a single, insular meaning become deeply problematic in a text that denies any credible answers and *Lot 49*'s ending is deliberately unsatisfactory, parodying romantic idealizations of the Modernist quest by halting in the middle of a sentence before the mystery is revealed. This next chapter is concerned with the ways in which *Lot 49* bases itself in a traditional novelist genre, but subverts the Modernist expectation of an ending of enlightened epiphanies. The text defers and postpones until any conclusive possibilities become ridiculous. Examination of this text shows that subversion of traditional genres and conclusions produces a stranger America, deviating from cultural representations of normalcy.

1. Tanner discusses this concept specifically in relation to Pynchon's first novel *V* in his significant book on American Literature, *City of Words*.

CHAPTER EIGHT

ILLEGITIMACY AND DISRUPTIVE IMAGINATION

A primary reason Oedipa is out of her depth has to do with historical issues—her suburban nineteen-fifties upbringing is ill-equipped to handle this new revolutionary atmosphere of the sixties. The San Narciso cultural environment conveyed through her middle-class eyes becomes progressively stranger as she is increasingly dislocated from the America she used to know, and lost in a new environment. Oedipa is the sole interpreter of changes in *Lot 49*, observing the radical shift in the conservative 1950s environment that transforms into the more radical sixties. The novel opens with her coming home from a Tupperware party, a quintessential suburban housewife activity[1]. As Nadel remarks in his indepth study of the decade, 1950s culture practiced and cultivated a cult of domesticity that aided in enforcing political and social containment (117). Typical housewife duties such as grocery shopping, watering the herb garden, and layering lasagna, emphasize the containment of Oedipa's desires and sexuality within the stifled suburban framework of Kinneret. *Lot 49* opens by situating us in these regular activities, but defamiliarizes the scene as well, juxtaposing it with a series of perplexing images—a door slamming in Matzalan, two hundred birds flying, Bartok's music concerto—all adding strange elements to an ordinary suburban scene (1). As Dugdale suggests, these images act as an estranging buffer zone, distancing Oedipa from the pull of Inverarity's will and San Narciso (127). Gregory Flaxman points out that this 'buffering' occurs from the very beginning of the novel when Oedipa's original suburban concerns are replaced by the mysterious Trystero (42). Oedipa attempts to understand Inverarity's letter, while almost defensively shielding herself by completing the rest of her housewifely duties:

> Throughout the rest of the afternoon, through her trip to the market in downtown Kinneret-Among-The-Pines to buy ricotta and listen to the Muzak...then

through the sunned gathering of her marjoram and sweet basil from the herb garden, reading of book reviews in the latest *Scientific American,* into the layering of a lasagna, garlicking of a bread, tearing up of romaine leaves, eventually, oven on, into the mixing of the twilight's whiskey sours against the arrival of her husband, Wendell ('Mucho') Maas from work, she wondered, wondered, shuffling back through a fat deckful of days which seemed (wouldn't she be first to admit it?) more or less identical, or all pointing the same way subtly like a conjurer's deck, any odd one readily clear to a trained eye (2).

Pynchon establishes Oedipa's Kinneret life as being nothing extraordinary before the interruption of Inverarity's letter. Attempting to understand Inverarity's summons while making lasagna, Oedipa demonstrates a desperate endeavor to juggle the old world which she grew up in, and the new world which is intruding into her life. In '"A Metaphor of God Knew How Many Parts":' The Engine that Drives *The Crying of Lot 49,*' Katherine Hayles expands on Dugdale and Flaxman's writing by providing telling examples of the protective layers that insulate Oedipa from reality. Hayles' examples of insulation include Oedipa, who 'couldn't feel much of anything' allowing Roseman to play footsie under the table with her boots (9); surrounded in 'musical ooze' while listening to Muzak in the supermarket (2), and layering lasagna, garlicking bread, and preparing whiskey sours, all activities contributing into numbing sensations against her husband arriving home from work. Hayles's illustrates how these examples of Oedipa's Kinneret activities have trained her to create this sense of 'buffering' or insulation from reality (102). Significantly, the layering upon layering of lasagna in Kinneret is contrasted with the slow unpeeling of clothes in the game of Strip Botticelli she plays after she is 'pierced' into reality by Inverarity's will in San Narciso.

Oedipa's perplexity and outsider status quickly projects her into strange situations in San Narciso. An early example occurs with Oedipa's uncanny vision in front of Echo Courts motel—the nymph's face advertising the motel is strikingly similar to her own (14). She is startled, not only by seeing her own image but by 'a concealed blower system' keeping the nymph's apparel in 'constant agitation,' revealing 'enormous vermillion-tipped breasts and long pink thighs at each flap' (15). The uncannyness of the vision derives from Oedipa recognizing something inherently familiar (herself) in the image, but made alien, increasing Shklovsky's 'difficulty and length of perception' (12). Oedipa is confronted by a perverted translation of the familiar 'Heim' into the unfamiliar, making her seem unfamiliar to herself and almost immediately after, stimulating thought on the slow whirlwind she had seen before, and straining to understand words she just couldn't hear (15). It is also significant that the lewd image confronts her at the beginning of her stay in San Narciso. Echo Courts motel is where she will be seduced out of her role as Kinneret housewife by Metzger, Inverarity's lawyer. Oedipa's promiscuous actions stray from her former domestic role as Mrs. Mucho Maas as she immediately launches into a drunken affair with Metzger.

As the novel progresses, Oedipa becomes more and more disoriented in her environment since: 'things then did not delay in turning curious' (28). The plot quickly progresses with Oedipa finding the pivotal Thurn and Taxis symbol at an electronica bar, launching her into an investigation into the historical inaccuracies of a thirteenth-century play, which becomes a general search for secret conspiracy in America. *Lot 49* significantly tells the tale of an American searching for meaning in America and, as mysteries unfurl, feeling disconnected and alienated from her own country. The desperate search for a meaning that retreats from the pursuer throughout the text confirms that Oedipa's story is not about the inheritance of Pierce's legacy or revealing the mystery of America but, as Bernard Duyfhuizen concludes, about her disinheritance and disenfranchisement, her casting out from the community as an American constructing an alternative narrative about America (93). Reading Oedipa's feelings of dislocation through Freud's Unheimlich theory, we see that her feelings of heim/unheim (home/unhome) are mirrored—not just in the opening pages of the novel—but throughout the entire text. San Narciso represents America and Oedipa is American, yet at the same time, the environment is alien and she is at a loss to reveal the concealed meaning in a city that 'did not have any vital difference between it and the rest of Southern California' (Pynchon 13). It does not surprise us in *Lolita* when Humbert is cast in an outsider's role in an American suburban neighborhood. What is extraordinary is the ease in which he infiltrates and enacts a role of belonging without detection of his fantastic desires. *Lot 49*'s contrasting narrative is about an American housewife, arriving in an environment no different from any other American city, but revealing astounding mysteries that alienate her into an outsider, driving her into paranoia:

> The repetition of symbols was to be enough, without trauma as well perhaps to attenuate it or even jar it altogether loose from her memory. *She was meant to remember.* She faced that possibility as she might the toy street from a high balcony, roller-coaster ride, feeding-time among the beasts in a zoo—any death-wish that can be consummated by some minimum gesture. She toughed the edge of its voluptuous field, knowing it would be lovely beyond dreams to simply submit to it; …she tested it shivering: I am meant to remember (87).

The passage's uncannyness derives not only from the unmistakable allusion to Freud's 'death-wish,' but from Oedipa's recognition that symbols or clues she sees *must* lead her in a sequential direction. This type of déjà vu feeling ('*She was meant to remember*') reemphasizes the uncanny feeling of 'remembering' and 'forgetting', 'familiar' and 'unfamiliar' or, 'home' and 'not home.' Oedipa's grasp of clues is founded on her upbringing, which has accustomed her to a linear narrative. This allows each clue to 'have its own clarity' relating to the previous clue so a coherent storyline is able to be properly constructed. Though Oedipa has no choice but to follow this narrative pattern, 'knowing it would be lovely beyond dreams to simply submit to it,' she is skeptical, doubting the legitimacy of what she is doing, listening to that niggling fear that 'the direct, epileptic word' is nonexistent, and thus, counterfeiting all narratives (87). The circumstances in San Narciso create the illusion of a once familiar environment transformed into an uncanny one. Oedipa's problem is that the physical setting of America has not changed but the linearity of America has now proven deceptive, leaving her adrift in 'the infected city' (86).

Oedipa has many of these ontological crises manifesting feelings of both uncannyness and alienation. David Sorfa has written one of the few papers that deal specifically with this topic. In '" Small Comfort": Significance and the Uncanny in *The Crying of Lot 49*', Sorfa notes a feeling of delirium, a fluttering that Oedipa feels, and later recognizes as occurring when she feels close to the possibility of a deeper revelation (Sorfa 79):

> She could, at this stage of things, recognize signals like that, as the epileptic is said to—an odor, color, pure piercing grace note announcing his seizure…Oedipa wondered whether, at the end of this (if it were supposed to end), she too might not be left with only compiled memories of clues, announcements, intimations, but never the central truth itself, which must somehow each time be too bright for her memory to hold;… (69)

Sorfa claims, interestingly, that Oedipa's brink of epileptic seizure is the most akin to Freud's 'Unheimlich' feeling. He suggests that Oedipa, feeling the possibility of such profound vision becomes excited into a physical trembling or 'Delirium Tremens,' creating an 'Unheimlich' state or uncanny feeling (79). This 'Delirium Tremens' concept is more specifically mentioned in Oedipa's empathetic observation of a sailor's death. The complicated metaphor is explored through the leaping of imagery and connections in Oedipa's mind in the much quoted passage where an unknown sailor dies in her arms. Oedipa firstly connects the loss of scientific information and facts with a man's personal tribulations and memories:

> She remembered John Nefastis, talking about his Machine, and massive destructions of information. So when this mattress flared up around the sailor, in his Viking's funeral: the stored, coded years of uselessness, early death, self-harrowing, the sure decay of hope, the set of all men who had slept on it, whatever their lives had been, would truly cease to be, forever, when the mattress burned (95).

Nefastis' machine is juxtaposed with the sailor's body, which also acts as a human information vessel, subsequently destroyed upon his death. The operative metaphor in Oedipa's paranoid reading of his death is found in the letters 'D.T.' signifying both 'delta,' the mathematical symbol for an infinitesimally smaller progression, and 'delirium tremens' or 'the shakes' when an addict attempts to stop taking drugs. Oedipa realizes this affliction in a moment of clarity:

> She knew, because she had held him, that he suffered DTs. Behind the initials was a metaphor, a delirium tremens, a trembling unfurrowing of the mind's

plowshare.
The saint whose water can light lamps, the clairvoyant whose lapse in recall is the breath of God, the true paranoid for whom all is organized in spheres joyful or threatening about the central pulse of himself...(95).

Oedipa's panoramic use of the 'DT' metaphor—religion, God, heroin shakes, and the mind—parallels her desire to believe an underlying order of meaning. The DT passage is an example of Oedipa connecting random signs, using this invented linear thread to act as a buffer, preventing realization that the text's cunning web of meanings that Oedipa senses everywhere is unsolvable or meaningless. DT symbolizes an infinitely smaller progression, just as Oedipa's hunt for more specific clues will never place her any closer to the central truth, it too acts as an infinitesimal progression of information. This is either an affliction she must deal with (like the shakes), or as Sorfa suggests, a path to transcendence through the means of almost religious enlightenment. Increasingly, Oedipa's obsessive probing at the teasing implications of metaphor and language excites her even as she is profoundly unsettled by her intuitions:

The act of metaphor then was a thrust at truth and a lie, depending on where you were: inside, safe, or outside, lost. Oedipa did not know where she was (95).

Sorfa argues that these close brushes with a larger understanding move Oedipa *almost* into enlightenment but, in the end, leave her unaltered. Oedipa draws close to revelatory understanding at several moments in the novel, looking for the 'profound word that might abolish the night,' and attempting to fabricate numerous clues into a larger pattern of meaning but never quite touching the numinous source of knowledge. She approaches ontological understanding from an outsider's point of view; everything is new and she is inexperienced in terms of dealing with this strange environment even though the physical landscape resembles that of every other major Californian city (13).

Sorfa argues somewhat unconvincingly that Oedipa's very nearness to an almost religious understanding is what pushes her into a delirious trembling, manifesting the uncanny dreamy atmosphere that is so vivid on her night journey (79). I believe that Oedipa's uncanny feelings can be explained more convincingly in metafictional language and less in ideas of religious enlightenment. Oedipa uncovers the possibility of a larger signified meaning out of a hodgepodge of clues, but already knows that these clues will never lead to the unveiling of a larger mystery. As Patricia Waugh has suggested, 'it is a concern with the idea of being trapped within someone else's order' and even more pertinently, 'trapped within language itself' (117-8). In *Lot 49*, we increasingly suspect that the signs and clues are already empty, any larger chain of significance curtailed by the underlying absence that Oedipa interprets as malign presence[2]. It is this failure of signification to point beyond itself to something ultimately real (all the while tempting Oedipa to look beyond the outward sign to some inner meaning), as well as the uncontrol that has overtaken the most familiar binary oppositions, that creates unfamiliarity. Under these circumstances, Oedipa's grasping towards the profound and her acute striving to formulate meaning produce not satisfaction, but a terrified apprehension of a nothingness she registers as a palpable presence:

> Each clue that comes *is supposed to* have its own clarity, its fine chances for permanence. But then she wondered if the gemlike 'clues' were only some kind of compensation. To make up for her having lost the direct, epileptic Word, the cry that might abolish the night (87).

This loss of meaning, for all its intimations of metaphysical loss, has a specifically American presence, local and ordinary. American surroundings, cultural artifacts and landscape seem to bear a weighty significance as Oedipa negotiates between her quest for ontological self-understanding and her desire to uncover the hidden plots determining contemporary American reality. She travels through an American landscape in which cultural signifiers leave her troubled, teased out of her familiar associations, yet devoid of understanding. Waugh observes that the only difference between literary fiction and reality is that the former consists entirely of language creating certain restrictions and limited freedoms (89). In the Delirium Tremens passage and in Oedipa's fraught self-examination in search of clues, the heroine of *Lot 49* is allowed to vaguely realize these literary restrictions[3], creating a strange and disquieting environment for the reader as well as the protagonist.

Oedipa's estrangement from her world is in part the outcome of a conscious decision: she chooses not to believe in the master narrative and constructs an alternative plot. Although her projection may not be any more legitimate than the official America she comes from, she realizes that she has no way back to its bland comforts. She accepts the new 'uncanny' nature of her country; any previous rationalizations of events are now forfeit. Much like Humbert, she reinvents America so as to gain access to alternate realities and permissive gaps within the master narrative. Oedipa's reinventions reveal the constructed nature of our consensual reality and how the smallest doubts can lead to an overturning of belief. She no longer believes in the master narrative, and therefore sees San Narciso with an outsider eye that is metaphysically unfamiliar. At the same time, the alternate community revolving around the Thurn and Taxis symbol is also unconvincing as a reflective world existing independently of our perceptions. As John Dugdale observes, academic writing has tended to side with the validity of Oedipa's 'revelations,' as most are inclined to 'read with Oedipa, rather than reading Oedipa' (126). Oedipa's questions are tinged with illegitimacy, one is left wondering whether the signs she see actually exist or are just a part of an increasing paranoia attributing meaning to random patterns and symbols of information. As Oedipa journeys through San Narciso, what she discovers is not whether there is an alternate underworld that is more legitimate than the surface reality, but the fact that *all* realities are illicit by nature. Sorfa points out that

'Oedipa's quest for the secret (the *heimlich*) results in a discovery of the *unheimlich* which is somehow also the homely (*heimlich*), the safe place' (81). Sorfa's view is unconvincing since none of Oedipa's worlds (Trystero, Post Office conspiracy, Invarity's elaborate Game, mental instability) are convincingly *Heimlich* or homelike, but are actually more *unheimlich* (unhome or Uncanny), as she begins to feel alienated in all universes. As Oedipa attempts to negotiate and improvise between worlds, she is constrained by being unconvinced and unconvincing as a reader caught between interpretations. Her disturbing questions in San Narciso manifest the vision of a stranger America, whose physical reality is questioned by illegitimate vision and disruptive imagination.

Lolita introduces us to a European outsider observing America from an immense distance, reimagining suburban America. At the same time, he manages to infiltrate America without detection. In *Lot 49*, main character Oedipas Maas is supposed to fit seamlessly into that society but doesn't. At the opening of Pynchon's novel we find Oedipa, a suburban housewife standing in her living room and feeling tipsy from too much kirsch at a fondue (3). The suburban family that Nabokov parodies in loving detail by the mid twentieth century was a cornerstone of American culture and identity. Humbert poses as an American father to blend into his new cultural surroundings and by his very success in doing so, renders the society itself strange. The narrative mechanics in *Lot 49* work in reverse. Native-born housewife Oedipa Maas has all the qualifications of belonging but remains emphatically out of place. A fantastic rendition of America is depicted through her domestic travels in her own homeland. Though she is native born, middle class and white suburban, Oedipa's perspective and vision of San Narciso is increasingly that of an outsider. She is what Linda Hutcheon deems 'excentric,' one who is inside and yet outside her culture (*A Poetics of Postmodernism*, 60)[4]. *Lot 49* begins with Oedipa receiving a letter in the mail summoning her to San Narciso to act as executor of Pierce Invarity's will. What follows is a vertiginous labyrinthine structure built around presumed hidden meanings, recurring symbols and dead end leads, all of which leaves Oedipa and the reader struggling for conclusion but unsatisfied.

Oedipa's home town of Kinneret is just two hours east, and she recognizes 'no vital difference' upon her first glance into San Narciso, but her arrival is still noticeably that of an outsider. Pynchon takes special care to describe the blinking unfamiliarity of her gaze:

> She looked down a slope, needing to squint for the sunlight, onto a vast sprawl of houses which had grown up all together, like a well-tended crop, from the dull brown earth; and she thought of the time she'd opened a transistor radio to replace a battery and seen her first printed circuit (13).

American, suburban, a product of the 50s—Oedipa should be unequivocally part of the normalizing discourse, but, instead, sees the irregularities in her own culture, journeying with a mixture of desperation and acceptance into what was formerly marginal but is now ubiquitous. This journeying allows her to participate in reinventing an alternate narrative in San Narciso, her life and upbringing in Kinneret beginning to seem more and more distant and strange.

Bernard Duyfhuizen[5] and Ann Mangel have drawn attention to the fact that Oedipa acts as an intermediary that negotiates a barrage of cultural information. Since Oedipa is sole mediator (her being the primary executor of Invarity's will is also significant), she is performing a double role of filtering information for the reader as well as attending to her own crisis of 'what to believe in' (81). Oedipa acknowledges the mystery is solvable—if only she could penetrate the code:

> Though she knew even less about radios than about Southern Californians, there were to both outward patterns a hieroglyphic sense of concealed meaning, of an intent to communicate. There'd seemed no limit to what the printed circuit could have told her (if she had tried to find out); so in her first minute of San Narciso, a revelation also trembled just past the threshold of her understanding (13).

Duyfhuizen observes that Oedipa falls into the tradition of 'storytellers,' meaning that using Inverarity's will as a foundation, she construct her own narration of events. However, Oedipa's problem is that she needs to be able to construct an *authoritative* narrative that satisfies both her and the text (82). Tanner reiterates these themes by referring to Oedipa as an unreliable 'cryptologist,' agonizing over legitimate interpretations of text, while trying not to invest an inordinate amount of personal interpretation (174). Oedipa's attempts at striving for objective scholarship are demonstrated in the incredibly detailed synopses of the film *Cashiered* and the play *The Courier's Tragedy*. Both abridgements are a point by point plot summarization, but significantly, through the selectively filtered consciousness of Oedipa from Kinneret. As the story progresses, our housewife remains an outsider to San Narciso, each of her bizarre experiences requiring more investigation and confounding her. This outsider status is crucial in defamiliarizing the landscape and casting authoritative doubt in her role as story teller. Oedipa's list of unfamiliar experiences include such wide ranging activities as investigating human bones in Fangoso Lagoons, attending the historically inaccurate and gruesome play *The Courier's Tragedy*, and finally, driving to Berkeley University in the middle of a protest and seeing it 'more akin to those Far Eastern or Latin American universities you read about...' (76).

From the very beginning, these destinations are defamiliarized, described through the eyes of someone (Oedipa) who does not belong to the large 'alternative' community taking shape in California. Petillon explains how Oedipa as main interpreter is well chosen from a naïve objective perspective as her consciousness is 'as ordinary as they come, being a 1950s housewife' (140). This ordinary consciousness is used effectively to interpret extraordinary surroundings. Oedipa's first impression of San Narciso significantly introduces her as an outsider, but acknowledges her familiarity as an American as well.

> San Narciso lay further south, near L.A. Like many named places in California it was less an identifiable city than a grouping of concepts—census tracts, special purpose bond-issue districts, shopping nuclei, all overlaid with access roads to its own freeway...But if there was any vital difference between it and the rest of Southern California, it was invisible on first glance (13).

In Narciso, there are no grouping of communities but only census tracts, districts and shopping malls that are owned by Inverarity and labeled as 'concepts.' John Dugdale suggests that Inverarity's economic monopoly over San Narciso may be the only tangible connection holding the entire city together (151). Oedipa, as executor of his estate, becomes therefore responsible for replacing him as the unifying force. Before Oedipa's arrival, San Narciso was indelibly stamped with Pierce Inverarity through a maze of money. Pynchon describes Inverarity as owning shopping centres, housing developments, freeway construction firms, cigarette manufacturers, theatres, Turkish baths, factories, retirement homes, including endowing the local college. Pierce's control over the city is ubiquitous and almost absolute, manifesting itself in a panorama of contemporary wealth and power that includes scenic as well as historical landscapes. Inverarity owns Fangoso Lagoons, but the water's history lies in the bodies of its dead soldiers, their bones dug up and used to make Beaconsfield cigarettes. Graveyards are plundered, facilitating mass highways, funded by the deceased investment mogul, still gathering profit beyond the grave. Inverarity's lasting legacy exudes death, creating a melancholy landscape that continues to dishonor the past, ransacking the remnants of national history for commercial gain.

Once in San Narciso, Oedipa attempts to use these same cultural artifacts, experiences, and memories to formulate what I refer to—and Dugdale supports this view—as a more meaningful landscape. This involves using artifacts and representations of American normalcy to formulate into a linear meaning, piecing finally into a grand commonsense narrative about her country. Oedipa is determined to translate San Narciso into an empathetic interpretation of America (Dugdale 127). By searching for the meaning of Trystero, part of what Oedipa is searching for is also self-realization, relying on clues that she finds in various San Narciso destinations. A large portion of her task involves reconstructing a San Narciso where 'bones still could rest in peace' without fear that anyone would 'plow them up' (72). Oedipa strives to create a more meaningful landscape 'in a land where you could somehow walk, and not need the East San Narciso Freeway...' (72). Using this technique, the vacuous reality of San Narciso is transformed into a pattern of potential meaning, conceivably about to be revealed by the 'crying' at the end of the novel. As the novel progresses, we begin to see that this longing for revelation is no longer adequate in face of the resistance of the strange new world she enters into. Oedipa's binary habits of thought are out of place in San Narciso, as well as the naïve expectation that she will find some tangible source of meaning. This ill-suitedness is amplified by the contradiction between Oedipa's attempted reinterpretation as well as the actual barrenness of the city. Oedipa's defamiliarization of San Narciso accomplishes Pynchon's purpose of upsetting our preconceived binary notions about America. Instead of grouping property concepts like Pierce, she substitutes with 'imaginative investment,' re-interpreting the San Narciso landscape, and seeking indiscriminately to once again, wrest the American Dream away from its sullied association with money and attach it to the purer purposes of the imagination (145).

1. For more in depth information, refer to Alison Clarke's book *Tupperware: The Promise of Plastic in 1950s America*. Clarke explains how the suburbs in the 1950s were targeted as 'tupperware picnic grounds for direct selling' (100).

2. Note the Derridean reference of the malign presence of logocentrism in the text.

3. One compares this to the landmark metafictional novel *The Comforters* by Muriel Sparks (1957) featuring a character that knew she was in a novel.

4. Pynchon's novels often revolve around 'excentric' characters that feel dislocated from America. See 'Pynchon's Early Labyrinths' and Hawthorne's discussion of Stencil in *V* (3).

5. Please see Duyfhuizen's article '"Hushing Sick Transmissions": Disrupting Story in *The Crying of Lot 49*.'

CHAPTER NINE

W.A.S.T.E. EVERYWHERE: PYNCHON AT THE MOVIES

Oedipa's attempts at a wistful representation of San Narciso contradict the present depiction of Inverarity's city, consisting of cultural and natural environments represented by strange technological imagery. The general landscape is often referred to in terms of technological circuitry, associating the human with the inanimate. The city further reverberates with an artificial glow like a printed circuit in a battery estranging Oedipa's already unfamiliar perspective. The contrast between the technological and natural San Narciso landscapes manifest unsettling qualities in the text. Pynchon often mixes the natural with the unnatural, creating strange landscapes and a surrealist backdrop for Oedipa to wander through and observe:

> They came in among earth-moving machines, a total absence of trees, the usual hieratic geometry, and eventually, shimmying for the sand roads, down in a helix to a sculptured body of water named Lake Inverarity. Out in it, on a round island of fill among blue wavelets, squatted the social hall, a chunky, ogived and verdigrised, Art Nouveau reconstruction of some European pleasure-casino. Oedipa fell in love with it. The Paranoid element piled out of their car, carrying musical instruments and looking around as if for outlets under the trucked-in white sand to plug into (37).

Oedipa, Metzger and the Paranoids arrive in tractors, which Pynchon characterizes as 'earth moving machines', technological apparatuses that artificially transform natural landscapes. The natural lake environment is renamed after Inverarity, a multimedia tycoon representing a corporate monopoly. Technological and artificial apparatuses frequently mediate between characters and natural landscape in *Lot 49*. The characters arrive noting the existence of the lake, but are more enamored with the giant casino next to it. The Paranoids arrive at the natural landscape and immediately search for outlets to plug their technological instruments into, as if unable to negotiate the natural without an artificial apparatus. Pynchon uses technological metaphors to negotiate natural landscape, thereby defamiliarizing the 'real' and producing an uncanny effect. Other examples of the artificial appropriation of natural landscape include the Lago di Pieta environment. The Paranoids describe it to Oedipa as a lake filled with human bones belonging to American soldiers that are dredged up to make American cigarettes (43). Nature and manufactured death have been joined indissolubly. In a similar example, Oedipa drinks dandelion wine with Genghis Cohen who picked the flowers years ago at a graveyard that is now a portion of the San Narciso highway (69). *Lot 49* abounds in artificial appropriation, biological scenery replaced by the manufactured, instilling a sense of unnaturalness in the environment.

Landscapes are artificially appropriated and also instilled with cinematic qualities, inducing further strangeness and an uncanny environment in San Narciso. This effect is compounded by a self-consciously metafictional quality in the writing as the novel is hyper-mindful of its fabricated status, its artifice. Driving to Fangoso Lagoons with the Paranoids, Oedipa and Metzger sweep past 'three-bedroom houses rushing by their thousands across all the dark beige hills' with the looming Pacific in the background, set up almost like a cinematic still shot (36). The narrator's reference to the 'sweep of three-bedroom houses rushing by' as they drive past induces cinematic comparisons of filmic cuts speeding through in a movie. The looming nature of the Pacific Ocean seems to counter all artificial appropriations which are referred to in the 'beach pads, sewage disposal schemes and tourist incursions' (37). To compound the strangeness of the passage, Oedipa and Metzger's encounter with this San Narciso landscape is filtered through an outside consciousness implicit in the narrative's description of the ocean:

> ...the unimaginable Pacific, the one to which all surfers, beach pads, sewage disposal schemes, tourist incursions, sunned homosexuality, chartered fishing are irrelevant, the hole left by the moon's tearing-free and monument to her exile; you could not hear or even smell this but it was there... (36-37)

This is one among many environments Oedipa visits in San Narciso that abound in lists of signifiers, empty cultural artifacts and dead objects in their description. This bric-a-brac of culture, as in *Lolita,* accumulates as an exhaustion of signifiers which result in what Tanner refers to as a 'dead landscape', where on every side there is a 'reassertion of the Inanimate'[1] (157). *Lot 49* is filled with dead landscapes from the opening pages of the novel with Mucho's second hand cars carrying an excess of debris, poignantly found in the 'actual residue of lives' being examined (4). The cars themselves smell 'hopelessly of children', each cultural artifact acting as a 'futureless, automotive projection of somebody else's life' (5). Oedipa describes 'clipped coupons lost, tooth shy combs', cultural artifacts acting as a direct representation of each displaced person. Mucho's greatest anxiety in his occupation is inferred by the concept that 'death' becomes 'no longer miraculous', each trade-in a 'dented malfunctioning version of himself' (5). The entire transaction was a mechanical process, yet the most 'natural' thing to do. This reinforces Patricia Waugh's concept of metafiction as Mucho's car lot and occupation no longer acts as a significant environment of work or action but as an exercise in artifice.

Anticipating Baudrillard's simulacra and Umberto Eco's hyperreal, Lois Tyson continues the discussion on how Pynchon's America proliferates as nothing more than a cultural bricolage of 'self-emptying commodity signs circulating in endless profusion' (5). This is mirrored in Oedipa's night journey; wandering the San Narciso streets and encountering the reoccurring post-horn symbol in the strangest of places, moving cyclically and getting nowhere closer to finding the truth. Oedipa's desire to make sense of her landscape and disordered semiotic world is not feasible in a country so exhausted with over-signification. The city is portrayed as 'sleeked' with customary images signified in brackets as 'cosmopolitan, culture, cable cars' (86-7). A man is described trying to ingest 'lotions, air-fresheners, fabrics, tobaccoes and waxes' in an attempt to assimilate all the 'promise, productivity, betrayal, ulcers, before it was too late;' (91). An over-abundance of signifiers saturates Oedipa's world so that it becomes excessively meaningful, and thus meaningless. Oedipa's binary habits of thought are out of place, as well as her naïve expectation that she will find some tangible source of meaning. Unlike texts where landscape only acts as a significant backdrop to the character's state of mind, in *Lot 49,* the environment itself participates—metafictionally—in Oedipa's rich semiotic narrative. This more active participation revolves around an idea of symbol searching in the landscape and an overindulgence of signifiers. Landscapes draw attention to themselves as artificial constructs as the natural is continually being appropriated by technology. Pynchon describes scene after scene, investing a lurid, almost surreal quality to the landscape as Oedipal pursues the recurring post-horn:

> And spent the rest of the night finding the image of the Trystero post horn. In Chinatown, in the dark window of a herbalist, she thought she saw it on a sign among ideographs. But the streetlight was dim. Later, on a sidewalk, she saw two of them in chalk, 20 feet apart. Between them, a complicated array of boxes, some with letters, some with numbers. A kids' game? Places on a map, dates from a secret history? She copied the diagram in her memo book. When she looked up, a man, perhaps a man, in a black suit was standing in a doorway half a block away, watching her (86).

With the configuration of the post-horn everywhere, San Narciso is transformed into a highly refined and artificial landscape. The recurrence of the post-horn at every turn invests the novel with a self-conscious quality that exacerbates the reader's as well as Oedipa's sense of estrangement. Oedipa imagines that she sees the post-horn on the glass window of a shop in Chinatown, but she cannot be sure as 'the streetlight was dim', casting doubt upon her visionary senses.

Next, she sees the horn clearly on a sidewalk in between a diagram of boxes and numbers. This seems promising as substantial evidence of a conspiracy, but 'a complicated array of boxes', letters, and numbers defeats her. Yet she still diligently copies down the diagram. Chalk-written letters and numbers on concrete remind Oedipa of children's hopscotch thus casting her credibility and reasoning powers in doubt as her belief in a true conspiracy is made still more fragile. Her sightings everywhere of the post-horn defamiliarize the entire scene, making arbitrary cultural artifacts (such as hopscotch) pregnant with meaning. At the same time, its proliferation of intimations of meaning produces unmeaning. The narrative is littered with an overabundance of signifiers, the most significant being this muted post-horn which Oedipa spots throughout the entire text. The post-horn transforms San Narciso into a weird environment, replacing familiar surroundings for Oedipa with increasing strangeness. Hall observes this uncanny feeling, writing that the reappearing post-horn contributes to Oedipa's fantastic night, 'possesses[ing] all the aura of dream and hallucinogenic experience' (70). The post-horn is literally stamped throughout the entire novel, investing the whole San Narciso landscape with potential meaning, which, in the end, remains unfulfilled. Tactics of defamiliarization used in landscape invest the novel with a transmogrified version of America where artificial appropriation, the inanimate and marginalized people take center stage. Dead landscapes are stamped with an alien symbol (the muted post-horn) showing that the environment self-consciously realizes itself as constructed, not attempting to forge a vested reality. These aspects defamiliarize the conservative fifties model of America and contribute in making it stranger.

As we move through the narrative, our sense of Oedipa as a shadow from the old world insinuating herself into the new one becomes more palpable. This is poignantly demonstrated in her desperate night journey through the streets of San Narciso. Oedipa fearlessly wanders the street, having been rendered almost nonexistent in the landscape and thus able to play at being both 'the voyeur and listener' (91). Her sense of unreality produces, in her mind, the effect of invisibility, and a sense of estrangement so profound that the physical world becomes transparent, unreal. She sees children that she stops believing in and who thus become imaginary (88); she passes by street gangs feeling no fear as 'perhaps [they] did not see her at all' (89). Oedipa becomes a kind of figuring of Jesus Arrabal's concept of 'another world's intrusion into this one' (88), a detached presence drifting through the real, translating its objects and entities into the imaginary. This invisibility reinforces her status an outsider not only in the world in general, but specifically in her own increasingly unreal country. Her stake in the official America of suburban ownership and sanctioned activities is dissipated as Oedipa becomes increasingly disenfranchised, pulled away from affiliation to nation in favor of the lost communities and individuals who inhabit the interstices of a disintegrating world.

Chris Hall substantiates this idea by pointing out that Oedipa's symbol search takes her into back alleys, deserted laundromats, graveyards and ghetto neighborhoods where she meets poverty-stricken outcasts, delinquents and minorities such as a Mexican girl who traces 'post-horns and hearts with a fingernail, in the haze of her breath on the window' (86). Descent from the world of Tupperware parties into these neighborhoods confirms that Oedipa's obsessive sense of mystery and Inverarity's will have taken her to another America wholly separate from her former middle-class housewife existence. The mystery of the horn—or rather her determination that some pattern or design lies behind the random signs that beguile and torment her—leads her to a defamiliarized America lying within or beneath her Kinneret environment, bringing her into closer contact with those that slip through the cracks of American wealth and inheritance, tangential to the main discourse. Dugdale affirms this by arguing that Oedipa's identification with the 'alienations/alien nations of San Francisco' stem from her calculated withdrawal from the primary narrative discourse (150). This is reinforced when Oedipa, by 'projecting a world', also projects herself into America's lost and forgotten inhabitants (Dugdale 135). Oedipa's inheritance from Inverarity is more like a *disinheritance* from the America she used to know as she becomes familiar with a transmogrified version that never existed before the appearance of the post-horn.

Intangible landscapes are infused with filmic qualities in *Lolita* that allow Humbert to achieve his fantastic desires. In *Lot 49*, Pynchon also uses filmic tropes and techniques, which will later be more extensively developed in *Gravity's Rainbow* and *Vineland*. In *Deep Surfaces*, Phillip Simmons makes a convincing case for Pynchon's later novels where everything in *Gravity's Rainbow* is filtered through film and in *Vineland*, filtered through television (164). All plot advancement and character interactions are mediated through the ironic eye of the camera. Simmons observes that the extensive allusions to and parodies of film in Pynchon's novels are 'a continual source of ironic deflection', generating his satire (164). Pynchon already begins to make use of this technique in *Lot 49* where we see increasing evidence of filmic influences and descriptive scenes that mimic shots from different camera angles. Landscapes are not translated into filmic realities as in *Lolita*, but actually *recorded* like a film in instant replay, fast forward, and a panoramic revolving of visual shots. The literary adaptation of the camera's restless, speeded up perspective creates a distanced and oddly dislocated narrative, as of someone always watching a series of frenetic scenes. This sense of anxious distance from a threatening disorder contributes to the atmosphere of paranoid schizophrenia that pervades the text. In *Fiction and the Camera Eye* Alan Spiegel discusses distance in the modern novel as 'the essential postulate of the camera's stance' (46). Oedipa's first view of San Narciso is from a big hill where her eye pans down from a distance as 'she looked down a slope...onto a vast sprawl of houses...' (13). Pynchon invokes the feeling of the sun glinting off a camera lens and reflecting onto the landscape, Oedipa 'squinting [because of] the sunlight' (13). During Oedipa's seduction at Echo Court motel, Metzger uses a combination of past screen and present persona, emphasizing that both are equally relevant in the representation of self. Metzger's movie *Cashiered* acts as the primary mediating factor between

Oedipa and Metzger during the advance of seduction. The action advances as the couple watch television commercials that are all Inverarity owned and eerily relevant to Oedipa. The domineering presence of *Cashiered* and Inverarity corporation commercials demonstrate the extent to which cinema and television have already begun to overwhelm American culture in the mid 1960s. Previously, we discussed the emergence of filmic tropes that characters in *Lolita* drew from and imitated in the 1950s. In Pynchon's 1960s, television and film have saturated culture to such an extent that the understanding of all reality is utterly mediated by film. Simmons discusses a world in *Gravity's Rainbow* based on film in which 'everyone sees reality with the filmmaker's eye' and 'the narrative continually employs cinematic techniques' to remind us that our understanding of this period is limited through film mediation (165). If the landscape in *Lolita* possessed filmic qualities, television and cinema have completely taken over in *Lot 49*. All characters and their understanding of self-identity are woven in through film and television references.

Cinematic tropes and images infect not only individual consciousness but also interpersonal relationships. Oedipa and Metzger's entire relationship is mediated by film, her first reaction upon meeting him is that someone was 'putting her on' as he resembles nothing so much as an actor (16). Reinforcing this impression, Metzger seduces Oedipa through the representations of himself on film. Each question that Oedipa asks about the film forces her to forfeit an item of clothing. It is telling that their orgasm coincides with an electricity blackout, illustrating the mediating presence of technology at every step of their relationship. This dependence on the filmic is parodied when Metzger explains that he is a former actor who has left the profession to be a lawyer. A mini-series is currently being made of his life starring ex-lawyer now turned actor, Manny Di Presso. Metzger explains the film's plot: 'an actor becom[ing] a lawyer reverting periodically to being an actor' (20). In Pynchon's America, there are no longer substantiated differences between film and reality, each relies on the other to explain individual identity and general history. Oedipa's striptease is synchronized with the couple's conversation about *Cashiered*'s plot; Metzger answers Oedipa in his child actor 'Baby Igor voice', where her 'beach ball' appearance alludes to nothing so much as slapstick television comedy (22). As his seduction progresses, the camera or 'filmic eye' in the text cuts in and out as Oedipa falls on Metzger and wakes up again 'to find herself getting laid'. This seems particularly bizarre as she arrives at a situation where she is already involved, described 'like a cut to a scene where the camera's already moving' (27). The camera weaves in and out of focus, complete with soundtrack music piped in by the Paranoids where Oedipa 'counted each electronic voice as it came in' (27). Oedipa counts the guitars 'till she reached six or so, and recalled only three of the Paranoids played guitars, so others must be plugging in' (27). This particular insight demonstrates Oedipa's acknowledgement of an alternative universe existing outside her control.

De Zwaalm endorses this in her reading of Pynchon novels as constantly embarking and expanding on what she refers to as the 'Life is A Movie' metaphor (83-84). Captivated by an old film of Metzger's on television, Oedipa responds to Metzger with the self-conscious ironic eye of film:

'Aha,' said Metzger, from an inside coat pocket producing a bottle of tequila.

'No lemons?' she asked, with movie-gaiety. 'No salt?' (19).

De Zwaalm further elaborates on the ontological implications of Oedipa's habit of thinking of her life as 'a movie, just perceptibly out of focus, that the projectionist refused to fix' (84). Not only does this support the view that Oedipa views herself as a fictional character directed by others, but more interestingly, it implies that 'her quest for Tristero is, of course, an attempt to bring this movie into focus herself' (De Zwaalm 84). This violation of the fictional boundaries conventionally agreed upon by subject and author contributes to the novel's consciousness of itself as artifice. In *Lolita*, Charlotte and Dolores draw upon cultural romantic tropes to dictate their attitudes towards interpersonal relationships. In *Lot 49*, Oedipa sees herself as if on film, listening to Metzger in his 'Baby Igor' voice and hearing the Paranoids' music piping in the background.

Simmons sees these filmic influences, which he refers to as 'the camera eye', as ironic external factors defamiliarizing the introspective reality of *Lot 49* (164). In the previously discussed Oedipa and Metzger seduction scene, Pynchon is doing what Robert Stam refers to as 'confound[ing] reality with spectacle' (32). Oedipa's acknowledgement of the artifice of her situation is an act of 'the novelist and the cineaste [here] unmask[ing] the contingent precariousness of the illusion generated by the play-world of their art' (29). In metafictional terms, we can describe Oedipa as realizing that the nature of her reality is artificially and *cinematically* constructed. The uncanny coincidence of Metzger as a child on television leads Oedipa to suspect that 'either he made up the whole thing' or 'he bribed the engineer over at the local station to run this, it's all part of a plot, an elaborate, seduction, *plot*' (the word plot, being particularly apposite here) (Pynchon 18). Oedipa has suspicions throughout the novel that often present themselves as paranoia. This paranoia manifests itself at times in the guise of the self-reflexive metafictional character, conscious of her own puppet status in the novel. Oedipa recognizes herself as belonging to a world that is an exercise in artifice, and the source of the 'design' that manipulates her increasingly uncontrollable life is at once economic (Inverarity's will), social (the lapse of America away from its utopian possibilities), cultural (the shift from the orderly fifties to the disintegrative sixties), and even metaphysical (behind the post-horn lies perhaps true meaning: the mystic's insight, the truth about the malign universe that Ahab seeks in the white whale). This participation of acting as if on film, allows Oedipa to recognize her world as an exercise in artifice, therefore defamiliarizing her reality, her situation, and the novel.

Oedipa's paranoid pursuit of her futile quest involves the reader in an increasingly unsettling experience of novel-reading. She comes to see everything as part of some complicated and ubiquitous plot and is unable to recognize a consensual reality. The agreement between the spectator (in this case the reader), and the subject (Oedipa), is broken when the subject no longer participates in a complicit reality. Waugh defines this kind of literary self-consciousness as 'the construction of an illusion through the imperceptibility of the frame and the shattering of the illusion through the constant exposure of the frame' (31). At many points in the novel, Oedipa is often on the brink of this realization, but is unable to completely clarify this feeling due to various instances of 'buffering' or reaching the edge of the frame and being brought back.

This buffering relates to Oedipa often maintaining a distance that Flaxman likens to 'watching a movie, just perceptibly out of focus, that the projectionist refused to fix' (20). *Lot 49* is full of this blurriness which Flaxman attributes to a gap between the two realities that Oedipa negotiates simultaneously (45). 'The world' in *Lot 49*, Flaxman argues, 'is perforated by such gaps' that are often supplemented by participating individuals who are able to negotiate the blurriness. This is demonstrated in the layering and buffering metaphors found throughout the text. Oedipa, however, becomes unable to negotiate the fissures in her apprehension of the external world; she experiences a 'muffled' feeling of sensory deprivation or blindness, indicative of her retreat behind obscuring protective screens. This self-insulation is referenced early in the book with Roseman's attempt to play footsie with a noncommittal Oedipa, and later with the multiple layers of clothing she wears in an attempt to outwit Metzger's seduction (8, 22). America for Oedipa is increasingly the blurred projection of a sequence of cinematic images which, far from attaching the Kinneret housewife to a recognizable or familiar reality, isolate and insulate her until she finds herself an actor in a game of strip Botticelli in San Narciso.

Oedipa's visual reception of America is also cinematic as she adopts the undiscerning eye of the camera. The human eye, Speigel explains, is selective as it can be 'fascinated' or 'inattentive' or 'obsessive' or 'absentminded' (66). Spiegel contrasts this human eye with the camera eye, regarding it as 'an eye that has been severed from a brain: a dumb eye' (66). The camera eye is unable to be discerning as it picks up the essential as well as the accidental and unessential, 'both held and coordinated, without distinction, in a single field of vision' (Spiegel 66). This cultivation of a passive oval of vision is demonstrated in the description of Oedipa's visit to the Yoyodyne Factory:

> Oedipa, behind her shades, looked around carefully, trying not to move her head. Nobody paid any attention to them: the air-conditioning hummed on, IBM typewriters chiggered away, swivel chairs squeaked, fat reference manuals were slammed shut, rattling blueprints folded and refolded, while high overhead the long silent fluorescent bulbs glared merrily; all with Yoyodyne was normal. Except right here, where Oedipa Maas, with a thousand other people to choose from, had had to walk uncoerced into the presence of madness (62-3).

Although Pynchon prefaces this passage with 'Oedipa looked around carefully', there is a contradiction here as her line of vision without moving her head could not be encompass the variety of office artifacts simultaneously, as well as the florescent bulbs on the ceiling glaring above her. This all-encompassing field of vision creates what Speigel defines as a kind of 'ocular loneliness', estranging her from her immediate surroundings (67). The Yoyodyne visit further emphasizes her 'distance' as Oedipa 'walk[ing] uncoerced into the presence of madness' is not Oedipa's own thought, but the observation of a distinct narrative voice; one that is affected by Oedipa's sensibility, but appears to have an external relationship towards the outside world. Previously, as Speigel explains, one could stand dumb before visual experience but always 'it [was] his visual experience before which he stands' (67). In *Lot 49*, Oedipa's astonishment is due to the 'shared method of cognition' with an outsider's eye that confounds and isolates her from her surroundings. This outside narrator conjoined to Oedipa's consciousness, acts in estranging her from her surroundings, and alienating her from the San Narciso environment.

As Hite and others have successfully argued, *Lot 49* follows the traditional pattern of a formulaic novel, deriving its main impetus from a presumably logical and explanatory ending. In following this pattern, Pynchon references not only principals of high modernist practices and traditional novels, but also the classic detective and mystery genres. The text religiously follows the structure of these traditional genres, but exposes the limitations of the conventions it employs through varying forms of parody. Filmic representations of reality also contribute to the defamiliarized environment by creating what Simmons describes as an ironic deflection of the scene (170). Different types of filmic and literary genres are parodied in *Lolita*, some parodies are even 'reparodied' and transformed into pastiche. In *Lot 49*, Pynchon works from a traditional novelistic structure to lull the reader into a false sense of reality before inverting the formula and surprising his audience. We are given a conventional modernist quest in Oedipa's search for tangible meaning in a legitimate mission to solve Inverarity's will. What defamiliarizes the structure and eventually the plot of the novel is that the quest increasingly moves away from the tangible into metaphorical realms of language, until we realize that a concrete realization of the motif is impossible.

The overabundance of information given—the synopsis of a twelfth-century play, a recipe for a scientific apparatus, the synopsis of a television movie, two sets of song lyrics—induces an instinctual need to organize the facts into some kind of logical sequence or coherent linear pattern. Our inability to successfully complete this task induces a mild form of paranoia in the reader that is comparable to Oedipa's mass paranoia and obsessions. For purposes of parody, Oedipa is deliberately caught in a novel that Pynchon organizes in terms of closure or in which release is achieved in the shape of a modern epiphany or an Aristotelian final cause—or at least the point at which these resolutions seem just about to be delivered. Oedipa's anxiety in the novel stems from this structural demand that she fulfill her final role which she is supposed to reach in the final conclusion of the novel. At first she is cautiously optimistic, sensing 'it seemed that a pattern was beginning to emerge, having nothing to do with the mail and how it was delivered' (64). She dutifully attempts to sort the multiple pieces of information and clues into a general order and logical coherence, hoping that 'another reading of that line might help light further the dark face of the world' (65). She is convinced that her pursuit of varying leads will result in a type of closure or release for 'there either was some Tristero beyond the appearance of the legacy America, or [there was] just America' (137). However, as her search continues and the excess of information is filtered through her consciousness, the quest moves increasingly away from such tangible realms as uncovering a 'secret', or 'solution', and more towards the conceptual realms of epistemology and language.

At inopportune moments in the text, the dual voices narrating *The Crying of Lot 49* reveal a contradiction of intentions. These uncertain discoveries and revelations frighten and confuse Oedipa. Viewing with an all-encompassing eye, the narrative voice sometimes acts in opposition to Oedipa's attempts to personalize and create the landscape of meaning she desires to inhabit. In Mexico City, Oedipa is so affected by Remedios Varo's *Bordando El Manto Terrestre* painting that she hoped her dark green sunglasses would 'seal around her sockets' and be 'tight enough to allow the tears simply to go on and fill up the entire lens space and never dry' (10). Oedipa attempts to come to terms with her ocular loneliness by reaching out and connecting with her surroundings 'carry[ing] the sadness of the moment with her that way forever' (10). Meaningful and tender landscapes are forged, temporarily at least, as Oedipa attempts to reach out and form consoling connections to her surroundings. She identifies with the maidens in the painting, weaving tapestries to fill the void of the world, unable to leave their environment. Tellingly, Oedipa realizes that the maidens (and she herself) are not made captive by the tower. What keeps them captive is a form of 'magic, anonymous and malignant, visited on her from the outside and for no reason at all' (11). This 'outside magic' has its physical presence felt in the filmic reality and narrative voice, which (frame by frame) records each scene for the reader/viewer. The reader comes to the distinct and metafictional realization that she is trapped as a character in a book, unable to formulate her own impact on the landscape and surroundings. If we think of *Lot 49* as an engaging metafictional narrative, it automatically becomes defamiliarized as a traditional conclusive genre. When we discussed filmic influences in the novel, De Zwaalm was mentioned explaining how Oedipa's attempt to solve the Tristero is a personal attempt to seize control of her own life from the 'projectionist' moving the film reel perpetually out of focus. Oedipa's self-determinism is seen as violating the rules of fiction, advancing into the realms of the more experimental genre of Metafiction. While embarking Oedipa on a Modernist quest following a very traditional genre, Pynchon at the same time reveals how her very pursuit of self-identity violates and defamiliarizes the boundaries of fiction.

One can refer to this in terms of narratological defamiliarization in which the character senses 'magic from the outside' or in other words, her status as an authored being. In that instance of baffled recognition of dependency and entrapment, Oedipa senses herself in the text, but a world in which she later finds out that her discovery of design brings no epiphany of sublimity or plenitude. We can further view this 'God' as the intuition of a governing principle behind reality and also (in Oedipa's nightmares) the apprehension of a malignity at the basis of being—not mere absence—but active negation, a purpose creating chaos and whirling all of us just beyond the limits of our knowledge. Realization of this helplessness early on in the novel estranges the clarity of her purpose with the knowledge that all conclusions reached are inadequate. Pynchon's strategies of defamiliarization in *Lot 49* are his attempts to combat this feeling of helplessness and binary thinking that were so prominent in the conservative 1950s. Ultimately, expressed metaphorically in the book, Oedipa's creations of meaningful landscapes and unfamiliar thinking are only able to accomplish a scant amount of difference in San Narciso, USA. Pynchon still regulates her as 'captive' and trapped in her metafictional universe.

Notes

1. Pynchon first introduces this concept in his novel *V* with the gradual artificial processing of the character 'V''s body until she is purely artificial.

CHAPTER TEN

'THE DIRECT APOCALYPTIC WORD':
DEFAMILIARIZATION AND BAKHTIN

Bakhtin refers to the technique of combining narrative voices—here an outsider consciousness and the inward thoughts of Oedipa—as a 'double voiced discourse', which attempts to conjoin two separate consciousnesses, interrelate, and have them dialogically interact with each other in a type of micrologue. Bakhtin explains that even if there is only a single consciousness involved in the narration of text, the novel still cannot be conceived as a 'monologic act' (249). In *Lolita*, other characters' heteroglossic voices are mostly heard in between Humbert's attempt at a monolithic narrative. In *Lot 49*, what emerges is not a polyphony of outside voices battling to be heard but *internal voices*, or, a 'battling' of divided voices within the narrator herself (Bakhtin 250). Such examples of internal dialogue occur throughout the novel, demonstrated in Oedipa's uncomfortable visit to the Berkeley campus, finding it 'akin to those Far Eastern or Latin American universities you read about' (76). The plaintive question, 'Where were Secretaries James and Foster and Senator Joseph?' and the mysterious answer, 'in another world', supports this idea of a micrologue at play between Oedipa and the narrator (76). The latter narrator very often (though not permanently or consistently) adopts Oedipa's perspective and language; or, more to the point, the language that at first glance appears to be narratorial often turns out to have originated with Oedipa after all. This is demonstrated in Oedipa's first impression and vision of San Narciso:

> There'd seemed no limit to what the printed circuit could have told her (if she had tried to find out); so in her first minute of San Narciso, a revelation also trembled just past the threshold of her understanding. Smog hung all round the horizon, the sun on the bright beige countryside was painful; she and the Chevy seemed parked at the centre of an odd, religious instant. As if, on some other

frequency, or out of the eye of some whirlwind rotating too slow for her heated skin even to feel the centrifugal coolness of, words were being spoken (13).

This figure of speech appears to emanate from the narrator, who captures Oedipa's state of mind in this figure but later on:

> She gave it up presently, as if a cloud had approached the sun or the smog thickened, and so broken the 'religious instant,' whatever it might've been; started up and proceeded...(12).

We discover that Oedipa is able to remember the religious instant as her own idea. Thus, 'the breaking up' of the religious instant is expressed in clearly Oedipal language: 'whatever it might've been; started up' again (13). Pynchon shows us here that the figure and realization actually emanate from Oedipa, and not from the narrator. This happens again in a more complicated fashion in the 'DT' passage, discussed earlier. This passage uses highly metaphorical language:

> The saint whose water can light lamps, the clairvoyant whose lapse in recall is the breath of God, the true paranoid for whom all is organized in spheres joyful or threatening about the central pulse of himself...(95).

moving into complicated imagery that involves language being expressed as imagery:

> ...the dreamer whose puns probe ancient fetid shafts and tunnels of truth all act in the same special relevance to the word, or whatever it is the word is there, buffering, to protect us from (95).

The DT metaphor is masked as the narrator's voice, but the thought seems to have originated with Oedipa as a couple of passages later she ponders her first memory of 'DT', 'screeching back among grooves of years' and taught to her by Ray Glozing, 'bitching among "uhs" about his freshman calculus' (95). In *Transparent Minds,* Dorrit Cohn discusses this duality of voice in more detail as 'psycho-narration', something separate from and more specific than the more general omniscient narrator. The psycho-narrator is often able to express dimensions of the character that the main character is unwilling or unable to self-narrate in the text (29). Thus, Pynchon deliberately blurs the boundaries between Oedipa and a separate higher consciousness, eschewing the monologic method. The conjoined voices that act as narration in *Lot 49* fall into the 'dual voice hypothesis' where narrative techniques as free indirect discourse combine 'the voice of a character with that of the narrator or superimpose one on the other' (McHale, *Routledge* 127). This is especially true in the small hours of the morning, after Oedipa has journeyed through the night and a wondering voice asks:

> Where was the Oedipa who'd driven so bravely up here from San Narciso? That optimistic baby had come on so like the private eye in any long-ago radio drama, believing all you needed was grit, resourcefulness, exemption from hidebound cops' rules, to solve any great mystery (91).

This passage, by using Oedipa's name in the third person, distinguishes the psycho narrative conscious as separate from Oedipa. As Cohn observes, passages showing psycho-narration tend to animalize or personify psychic forces. Phrases such as 'optimistic baby' and 'hidebound cops' rules' tend to give a vague objective persona to the external consciousness. This psycho-narrator often expresses the contradictory and complicated nature of Oedipa's thoughts and feelings. We read on and find the narrator answering his/her own rhetorical question about Oedipa:

> But the private eye sooner or later has to get beat up on. This night's profusion of post horns, this malignant, deliberate replication, was their way of beating up. They knew her pressure points, and the ganglia of her optimism, and one by one, pinch by precision pinch, they were immobilizing her (91).

There is deliberate disjuncture here between the narrator's idioms ('malignant', 'ganglia') and Oedipa's own speech in moments of crisis.[1] However, these thoughts that were separate from Oedipa, immediately meld into her own consciousness as she thinks specifically of how she has seen each and every posthorn stamped everywhere, speculating self-consciously on an army of 'God knew how many citizens, deliberately choosing not to communicate by U.S. Mail' (92). As Bakhtin states, '[a] voiceless and accentless fact is presented in such a way that it can enter the hero's field of vision and can become material for his own personal voice' (251). By picking up on the rhetorical plea of the external narrator and fusing the queries into her own thoughts, Oedipa demonstrate the sinuous back and forth internal micrologue that exists between the two voices.

Double-voiced constructions, especially the fluid and elusive types that one finds in *Lot 49*, continually defamiliarize our notion of language as single-sourced—as emanating from one and only one consciousness at a time, one and only one position. Bakhtin refers to it as 'authorial discourse' and explains that it can never ultimately 'encompass the hero and his word on all sides, cannot lock in and finalize him from without. It can only address itself to him' (251). We have seen evidence of this self-addressing micrologue between the back and forth dual narration of Oedipa and a higher voiced consciousness that consistently confuse the idea of thought ownership and perspective. Ultimately, as Bakhtin argues, such constructions defamiliarize our assumption that we 'possess' our language, that it is 'ours'. In fact, says Bakhtin, 'our' language is always collective, always somebody else's as well as our own; it always comes from elsewhere, not from within. And this insight runs counter to all our prejudices about language.

1. Near the end of the novel, as Oedipa has a moment of crisis of what to believe in, she addresses herself with the words 'you are a nut, Oedipa, out of your skull' (128). This acts as a remarkable counterpoint of language difference to the psycho narrator's self-addressment.

FINAL REMARKS

What doesn't make strange, estrange, strangify a book if the author is a genuine artist?

—Vladimir Nabokov

In an interview with the *Paris Review*, Nabokov was questioned about the validity of a prominent critic who had dismissed his novels as 'extremely repetitious'. Never predictable, Nabokov answered, 'he may have something there. Derivative writers seem versatile because they imitate many others, past and present. Artistic originality has only its own self to copy' (5). This book ends with these two quotes from Nabokov because they reiterate the reasons I have chosen these two authors to situate this book on defamiliarization. Both Nabokov and Pynchon follow this kind of artistic originality in their writings by alluding directly to their own work in subsequent novels, and by creating strange worlds out of the ordinary. These more intense versions of our own worlds allow us an avenue into reassessing habitual perceptions in our own lives, and what we have taken for granted enchants us after reading we are left restless, with disturbing questions that only arise after reading such unsettling literature.

Lolita's originality lies not only in its subject matter, but in its ability to enchant and enamor in spite of the insidious nature of content. *Lolita* makes us believe in the nature of love again, it renews one of the most readdressed subjects in Western Literature by inventing new ways of imagining its incarnation. Nabokov accomplishes this feat by not only inventing a delightfully enchanting portrait of an American pre-teen, but enfolding us in her American world, transcribing the vulgar signage and slang language, stimulating us further by description that, at times, rises into metaphorical flights of poetic beauty. Ordinary routines, cultural artifacts and landscapes are listed, described, and made innocuously strange and beautiful, seducing us anew and making us believe and support Humbert's reinvention of America.

Lionel Trilling has written quite famously, that '*Lolita* is not about sex, but about love'. In a somewhat defensive justification, he further explains that 'almost every page sets forth some explicit erotic emotion or some overt erotic action and still it is not about sex. It is about love' (5). *Lolita* is about love, and Humbert's love of America and Lolita, but this is love for a girl reinvented, and an America defamiliarized. Humbert's narration is driven by his need to reinvent a 'dreamy large country' that obscures his perversity and exempts him from moral reprehensibility. This is accomplished through the defamiliarizing of suburban place, making one's familiar home seem strange or uncanny, as well as conveying a cinematic landscape, rendering his actions inculpable. It is not a coincidence that Humbert compares the American natural landscape to the last frontier and describes Quilty's murder in a combination of slapstick imagery and Western action prose. The other characters themselves are rarely able to speak, Humbert often anticipating their unsaid thoughts and actions including most significantly, Dolores Haze. We have discussed how even in Humbert's climactic final meeting with her, Dolly's words remain lost and Humbert invents her speech. However, Nabokov undermines Humbert and deliberately allows traces of Lolita to flutter through Humbert's controlled narrative. Thus we have levels of defamiliarization involving Humbert as well as an undermining of narratorial intentions acted on by the author. Linguistic deviance is revealed in the contrast between Humbert's highly metaphorical descriptions of Lolita juxtaposed with Dolores' unpleasant rudeness. Dolores' voice is slight compared to Humbert's lush prose, but exists as an abrasive contrast to render Humbert's verbal world strange. I mentioned 'Poshlust' previously, defined as bad taste which disguises itself as something true or beautiful. We can identify in Nabokov's term a general metaphor for Humbert's 'confessional' narrative and love for Lolita. Humbert disguises his love for Lolita as something great through the archly metaphorical language of the novel and the re-invention of the Americans that he meets in their country. What Humbert's love actually is, as Wood explains, is something quite different, something more akin to his 'ramblings and blind convulsions' (123). While Humbert defamiliarizes America to escape moral reprehensibility, what the text covertly accomplishes is the defamiliarization and ultimate transformation of Humbert's poshlust into respectable love.

In many ways, the 1950s American containment culture with its perfection of domestic veneer mirrors our narrator's intensely detailed enclosure, whose all-encompassing love almost suffocates. Irena Smith elegantly suggests that Humbert and Dolores's transcontinental journey in *Lolita* acts as an eloquent allegory for one of the key motifs in the book: 'the transformation of the classically American sprawling spaces and open road into an insular, inward-looking universe' (88). Humbert is the outsider that dictates and narrates, altering our perception of events, landscape, and characters by his unnoticed presence in America. He acts as Schlovsky's defamiliarized eye: lengthening our perceptions of common images that become untoward and alien to our awareness so that we view them as new, deautomatizing our perceptions of their existence.

Uncanny situations are not created in both novels, but transcribed from the normal into the strange. Such ordinary activities as mowing the lawn or driving the car are given an element of strangeness by our outside narrator performing those mundane tasks. Girls skipping ropes, reading comic magazines, lists of American cultural artifacts all clump into extended paragraphs; landscape infused with the cinematic makes America a changed and unfamiliar world that, we not only love anew but cherish because of the erudition and metaphor of our pedophilic narrator. In *Lot 49*, Oedipa's strange sense of dislocation is founded on the brink of realization—not of finally finding meaning but that her world is meaningless. Such paranoid fantasies as recurring hieroglyphic symbols in landscape, an underground postal system, secret codes in an obscure thirteenth-century play are all unreliable truths, but provide Oedipa's only basis for reality. Oedipa's experiences, the cultural artifacts that catch her eye and obsess her and the people that she interacts with all make America foreign and place her in an uncanny interaction with her own country.

Pynchon places us in an empathetic understanding with Oedipa's alienation in America. Oedipa's world has altered focus—she is no longer in complete control of her reality and feels increasingly unsure of being a reliable interpreter of events that rapidly increase in strangeness. She is charged with the responsibility of being the only link that holds San Narciso together, and so attempts to forge together a narrative that is meaningful and coherent, a landscape that invests the entire city with potential meaning that can be knitted into a resolved story. Instead, she becomes more and more disenfranchised from her country, the clues she uncovers leads her further away from a satisfactory ending, uncovering possibilities that funnel in different directions. Instead of advancing in her mystery, she stagnates, retreats in different directions and becomes lost, never finding 'the direct apocalyptic word'. This is demonstrated in her symbol searching throughout the novel, where a muted post-horn is found stamped throughout the various scenes in the book—scrawled against a wall, on a scrap of paper, in a woman's washroom stall, traced by a girl in steam on a bus window. The muted post-horn is the singular clue that reoccurs repeatedly in the landscape, accomplishing little save contributing to the artificial and synthetic nature of her environment. The presence of the muted post-horn invests the most arbitrary artifacts with potential meaning, left unresolved for us and Oedipa as she waits in vain for 'the crying of lot 49' on the last page of the book.

Similarly, Humbert is on a mission to invent and reinvent America into a place fantastic enough to make his desires permissible. Natural landscape is defamiliarized through the infusement of cinematic imagery and the commercial appropriation of advertisement. Humbert cannily mentions Wild West movies, gun shootouts and Southern Belles to equate his own situation with the unrealistic and forgivable environment of the movies, thereby excusing him from moral culpability. His descriptions of landscapes leap from prehistoric imagery to gas station confetti. The Wild West he describes romanticizes violence and love, both of which are also vivid in his affair with Lolita. She herself is no longer

Dolores Haze, coerced and bullied into becoming his metaphorically more enchanting Lolita who is his constant companion for two years where he trespasses through and reinvents that 'lovely, trustful, dreamy, enormous country' (186).

By the time we reach *Lot 49*, cinematic involvement and film have already been established in the environment to the point of saturation. Characters pretend that they are in a movie, reality and film are so completely intertwined that Oedipa's seduction is mediated by Metzger's movie, and she addresses him in her imagined movie dialogue. Filmic influences are evident in camera angles that pan the landscape but also in Oedipa's acknowledgement of the Paranoids piping in among the background, joining amidst other guitars that are already playing. Oedipa plays with the idea of 'life as a movie' dimly realizing that the contrived nature of film juxtaposes with the artificial nature of her reality as a character in a book. The text 'bares the device', calling attention to itself as artifice and causing estrangement. Pynchon's playing with ideas of contrived reality is mirrored in the artificial quality of San Narciso's landscape. A mix of the technological and the natural is created in many of the landed highways lined with motel upon motel and census tracts that dot the city like glowing batteries. The next scene, however, has the insurmountable looming ocean closing in on Oedipa and Metzger traveling in the car, the Paranoids jump out at the beach but feel perplexed as they have nowhere to plug in their electric guitars. The Paranoids hope to repeat their soundtrack performance at the motel, but the natural environment resists them the way that Echo Courts Motel environment did not. The dominating filmic influence in *Lot 49* creates an extremely artificial landscape, Oedipa in particular realizing that something is amiss, perhaps even contrived. The landscape becomes no longer significant, but an exercise in artifice when Oedipa vaguely realizes that she is being controlled by an outside entity. Oedipa's affectation of 'being in a film' forces her to realize the contrived nature of her reality, ultimately, defamiliarizing her situation and the novel.

The conjoining of artificial and the natural is present not only in the description of scenic landscapes and environments but also in the depiction of people that become stock characters, already precedent as cliché in Humbert's narration. Humbert's reduction of everyone he meets in America to flat parodies (this includes Charlotte and Lolita), diminishes them as empathetic characters and reduces the atrocity of his moral outrages against them. However, this plan often backfires and the characters that he so dismissingly sneers at, lash out unexpectedly against him; Humbert finds out that 'they are as real as he is and often have plans of their own' (Boyd 250). No matter how strenuously Humbert attempts to control the text, characters subvert his intentions, 'McFate' often standing idly by ever ready to surprise him. A structural way in which this often happens is through the inversion of different types of genre throughout the novel. Nabokov's layout of filmic and literary structures such as romantic, buddy/pal roadtrip, and 'the double' acts almost like a trap as he unexpectedly defamiliarizes our expectations of their conclusion by inverting them. Humbert becomes his own double as he pursues Quilty and Lolita, Lolita is his romantic invention, but she runs away from him and instead of him acting as the seducer, she seduces him in The Enchanted Hunters Motel, no longer a virgin.

Dual voice narration or the microlologue between the empathetic narratorial voice and Oedipa also contribute to defamiliarization in *Lot 49*. The blending of consciousness between the two narrators problematizes our traditional conceptions of language as single sourced. Though it is quite clear to us that most of the narration is voiced and filtered through Oedipa (such as the summarization of *The Courier's Tragedy* and *Cashiered*), an outside, almost omniscient narrator breaks through with clearly different language. Similarly, Humbert's dictatorial attempts at mastering linguistic control over the entire text often falls short, with Charlotte parodying his words back at him in their final confrontation and Lolita every now and then expressing an intellect and wit that runs counter to his portrait of her character. In *Lolita*, Nabokov demonstrates that language is not monolithic but polyphonic as heteroglossic voices often color the text with discord while in *Lot 49*, Pynchon demonstrates that language and consciousness are multi-sourced, running counter to all our prejudices about language.

In 'Wakefield', Nathaniel Hawthorne tells the tale of a man who one day decides to leave his wife with no explanation and take up secret residency in a neighboring house for the next twenty years. Then, one day, he decides to move back into his original house with no explanation. The short story offers multiple possibilities as to why the man would commit an action that creates such discontinuity in his life, all falling short of Hawthorne's last sentence which simply states that 'by stepping aside for a moment, a man exposes himself to losing his place forever'(20). Tanner explains in *City of Words* that this idea of stepping out of society and 'into the void' is what motivates American heroes in fiction to continue the search for freedom and reality (30). We can consider Oedipas Maas as one such heroine who leaves her housewife existence in Kinneret, hoping to return, but in actual fact, 'step[s] into the void' and loses her place, slipping amidst the cracks and margins of America society. The environment is defamiliarized, thanks to the new transient nature of the main character that begins to view her home in an unfamiliar manner due to her losing her place forever.

In *Lolita* Humbert invents an America that is more to his taste whereas in *Lot 49* Oedipa loses touch with her reality. Both novels question our everyday perceptions and prejudices by disturbing our sense of equilibrium in their fictional techniques, the questions they raise, and also in our language they exercise with such skill. We are left with one of the final revelations of Oedipa Maas:

> Suppose, God, there really was a Tristero then and that she *had* come on it by accident. If San Narciso and the state were really no different from any other town, any other estate, then by that continuity she might have found the Tristero anywhere in her Republic, through any of a hundred

lightly-concealed entranceways, a hundred alienations, if she'd looked. (135)

The Crying of Lot 49 and *Lolita* teach us to *look* as readers by reinventing our known worlds into the unfamiliar, challenging us to reassess our minimal everyday perceptions and more strenuously engage in authenticating the world around us.

BIBLIOGRAPHY

Appel, Jr., Alfred: '*Lolita*: The Springboard of Parody'. *Vladimir Nabokov's Lolita: Modern Critical Interpretations.* (ed. Harold Bloom). New York: Chelsea House Publishers 1987, pp. 35-52.
Bader, Julia. '*Lolita*: The Quest for Ecstasy'. *Crystal Land: Artifice in Nabokov's English Novels.* Berkeley, CA: University of California Press, 1972, pp. 57-81.
Bakhtin, M.M. *Problems of Dostoevsky's Poetics.* Minnesota: University of Minnesota Press,1984.
Bloom, Harold. 'Introduction.' 'Vladimir Nabokov's *Lolita*: Modern Critical Interpretations' (ed. Harold Bloom). New York: Chelsea House, 1987, 5-12.
Boyd, Brian. *Nabokov: The American Years.* New Jersey: Princeton University Press, 1993.
Brand, Dana. "The Interaction of Aestheticism and American Consumer Culture in Nabokov's *Lolita*." *Modern Language Studies* (Potsdam, NY), Spring 1987, 17:2, pp. 14-21.
Clarke, Alison J. Tupperware. *The Promise of Plastic in 1950s America.* Washington: Smithsonian Institute Press, 1999.
Cohn, Dorrit. *Transparent Minds: Narrative Modes for Presenting Consciousness in Fiction.* New Jersey: Princeton University Press, 1978.
Colville, Georgiana M.M. *Beyond and Beneath the Mantle: On Thomas Pynchon's The Crying of Lot 49.* Amsterdam: Rodopi Editions, 1988.
Cowart, David. 'Pynchon and the Sixties.' *Critique: Studies in Contemporary Fiction.* 41:1 (Fall 1999): 3-12.
Davydov, Sergej. 'Poshlost.' *The Garland Companion to Vladimir Nabokov.* New York: Routledge Press, 1995. 628-31.
De Zwaan, Victoria. *Interpreting Radical Metaphor in the Experimental Fictions of Donald Barthelme, Thomas Pynchon, and Kathy Acker.* New York: The Edwin Mellen Press, 2002.
Derrida, Jacques. *Of Grammatology.* Trans. Gayatri Chakravorty Spivak. Delhi: Motilal Banarsidas Publishers, 2002.
Dugdale, John. *Thomas Pynchon: Allusive Parables of Power.* New York: St. Martin's Press,1990.
Fitzgerald, F. Scott. *The Great Gatsby.* London: Penguin Books, 1990.
Flaxman, Gregory. 'Oedipa Crisis: Paranoia and Prohibition in *The Crying of Lot 49*' *(41-58).Pynchon Notes.*

Frosch, Thomas R. 'Parody and Authenticity in Lolita.' *Modern Critical Views: Vladimir Nabokov* (ed. Harold Bloom). New York: Chelsea House Publishers, 1987. 127-142.

Hall, Chris. 'Behind the Hieroglyphic Streets, Pynchon's Oedipa Maas and the Dialectics of Reading'. *Critique: Studies in Contemporary Fiction.* 33:1 (Fall 1991): 63-78.

Hawthorne, Nathaniel. 'Wakefield.' *The Portable Hawthorne.* New York: The Viking Press, 1969.

Hayles, N. Katherine. 'A Metaphor of God Knew How Many Parts.' Ed. Patrick O' Donnell. *New Essays in the Crying of Lot 49.* New York: Cambridge University Press, 1991.

Hite, Molly. *Ideas of Order in the Novels of Thomas Pynchon.* Columbus: Ohio State University Press, 1983.

Hollander, John: 'The Perilous Magic of Nymphets'. *Partisan Review* (New York), 23:4 (Fall 1956): 557-560.

Hutcheon, Linda. *The Politics of Post-Modernism.* New York: Routledge Press, 2002.

Jameson, Frederic. 'Periodising the Sixties.' (ed. Patricia Waugh). *Postmodernism: A Reader.* London: Hodder and Stoughton Press, 1992.

Jameson, Frederic. *Postmodernism: Or the Cultural Logic of Late Capitalism.* Durham: Duke University Press, 1991.

Marling, Karal Ann. *As Seen On TV: The Visual Culture of Everyday Life in the 1950s.* Cambridge: Harvard University Press, 1994.

Masschelien, Anna. 'A Homeless Concept Shapes of the Uncanny in Twentieth-Century Theory and Culture'. *Image and Narrative.* http://www.imageandnarrative.be/uncanny/anneleenmasschelein.htm

McHale, Brian. *Postmodernist Fiction.* New York: Methuen Press, 1987. 'Dual Voiced Hypothesis' *Routledge Encyclopedia of Narrative Theory.*(ed. David Herman, Manfred Jahn and Marie-Laure Ryan). London: Routledge Group, 2005.

Nabokov, Vladimir. *Lolita.* London: Random House, 1992.

———. *Lectures on Literature.* New York: Harcourt Brace Jovanovich, 1980

Nadel, Alan. *Containment Culture: American Narrative, Postmodernism, and the Atomic Age.* Duke University Press, 1995

'Nosepicking Contests.' *Time.com*___6 May 1966. Time Inc., 2006 http://www.time.com/time/magazine/article/0,9171,901889,00.html

Olsen, Lance: *Lolita: A Janus Text.* New York: Twayne, 1995.

Petillon, Pierre-Yves. ;A Re-cognition of Her Errand into the Wilderness.' Ed. Patrick O' Donnell. *New Essays on The Crying of Lot 49.* New York: Cambridge University Press, 1991.

Pynchon, Thomas. *The Crying of Lot 49.* Toronto: Bantam Books, 1966.

———. *Slow Learner: Early Stories.* Boston: Little Brown, 1984.

Shklovsky, Victor. 'Art as Technique.' *Russian Formalist Criticism: Four Essays* Ed. Lee T. Lemon and Marion J. Reis. Lincoln: University of Nebraska Press, 1965.

Sorfa, David. ' "Small Comfort:" Significance and the Uncanny in *The Crying of Lot 49*'. (ed. John M Craft). *Pynchon Notes* Spring-Fall 1993 # 32-33.

Simmons, Phillip E. *Deep Surfaces: Mass Culture and History in Postmodern American Fiction.* Georgia: University of Georgia Press, 1997.

Smith, Irena Auerbach. 'A Garden and a Twilight, and a Palace Gate": Plotting the Intersection of Europe and America in Henry James's *The Portrait of a Lady* and Vladimir Nabokov's *Lolita*'. *Pacific Coast Philology*, Vol. 34: 1 (1999): 80-95.

Sparks, Muriel. *The Comforters.* London: Macmillan Press, 1957.

Spiegel, Alan. *Fiction and the Camera Eye*. Charlottesville: University of Virginia Press, 1976.

Stam, Robert. *Reflexivity in Film and Literature: From Don Quixote to Jean-Luc Godard.* New York: Columbia University Press, 1992.

Stark, John O. *The Literature of Exhaustion: Borges, Nabokov, and Barth*. Durham: Duke University Press, 1974.

Tanner, Tony. *City of Words*. London: Jonathan Cape Ltd, 1971.

Tweedie, J. '*Lolita* Loose Ends: Nabokov and the Boundless Novel.' *Twentieth Century Literature*, 46:2 (Summer 2000): 150-170.

Tyson, Lois. 'Existential Subjectivity on Trial: *The Crying of Lot 49* and the Politics of Despair'. *Pynchon Notes*. Spring-Fall 1991 28-29. 5-25.

Waugh, Patricia. *Metafiction: The Theory and Practice of Self-Conscious Fiction*. London: Methuen and Co, 1984.

Williams, William Carlos. 'To Elsie'. *Selected Poems*. New York: New Directions Books, 1968.

Wood, Michael. *The Magician's Doubts*. Princeton University Press, 1997.

Wyllie, Barbara. *Nabokov at the Movies: Film Perspectives in Fiction*. London: McFarland and Company, Inc, 2003.

INDEX

A

advertise, advertising, xi, 11, 31
artificial, xi, 15, 16, 29, 35, 59-62, 65, 71, 76, 77
american dream, 56
Annabel, 7, 30
Augustine, Augustinean, 43

B

Bader, Julia, x
Bakhtin, M.M., v, 30-32, 37, 71, 73
Baudrillard, Jean, 61
Betty Crocker, 42
Brand, Dana, 33, 34
Boyd, Brian, 3, 7, 19, 35, 78
buffer, buffering, 47, 48, 51, 66 72

C

camera, 63-66
Cashiered, 54, 63, 64, 79
cinema, cinematic, Hollywood, vii, ix, xi, 15-16, 17, 18, 23, 27, 43, 60, 64, 65, 66
Cohn, Dorrit, 72, 73
comic book, 15, 23, 26, 27
Cohn, Dorrit, 56, 57
Courier's Tragedy, The, 43, 54
conspiracy, 43, 62
culture, american, vii, xi, 4, 29, 47
    counterculture, 42, 43

parody of, 15, 31, 36
surburban, see surburbia,

D

defamiliarization
    development of, ix, xi, 3, 4, 24, 71
    environment, x, 7, 11
    landscape, 58, 62
    language, 31, 34, 36, 37
    literary, 15, 68
detective, 23, 26, 27, 67
delirium tremens, DT, 50-52
De Rougement, Dennis, 3
De Zwaalm, Victoria 64, 65, 68
domesticity, domestic, 9, 10, 18, 42, 47, 48, 53
Duyfhuizen, Bernard, 49, 54
Dugdale, John, 52, 55, 39

E

Eco, Umberto, 61
Emerson, Ralph Waldo, 43
epiphany, 67, 69

F

father / daughter, 23, 24, 26
fetish, fetishizing, 19, 20, 30, 36
Fitzgerald, F Scott, 53
Flaxman, Gregory, 47, 48

Freud, Sigmund, xi 7, 8, 13, 49, 50
Frosch, Thomas, 24, 25, 26

G

genre, ix, xi, 21, 23, 24, 26, 27, 28, 46, 67, 68
Ginsberg, Alan, 41

H

Hall, Chris, 62
Hayles, Katherine, 48
heteroglossia, heteroglossic, xi, 30
Hite, Molly, 67
Hutcheon, Linda, 32, 37, 53

I

insider, xviii, ix, 8, 34
interpreter, 42, 54

J

Jameson, Frederic, 27

K

Kerouac, Jack, 41

L

language
    american english, 30
linguistic, 24, 27, 30, 31, 32, 35, 36
    slang, 29, 30, 31

M

Mangel, Ann, 54
manichean, 43
Masschelein, Anneleen, 17-18
Marling, Karol Ann 9, 11
mcFate, 27

McHale, Brian, 30, 72
mediator, 54
metafiction, metafictional, 53, 60, 61, 65, 68, 69
modernism, modernity, 44, 67, 68
moral, Morality, x, xii, 4 , 17, 20-22, 26, 33, 34, 35
movies, film
Nabokov, 21, 27, 33
Pynchon, 60, 63, 64-66, 67

N

Nabokov, Vladimir
    Ada, 26
Nadel, Alan, 47
nostalgia, nostalgic, 17
nymph, Nymphet, Nymphetmania, 4, 10, 35, 30, 34

O

Oedipus Rex, 43
Olsen, Lance, 34
ontology, ontological, 50, 51, 52
outsider, 4, 9, 10, 12, 15-17, 33, 34, 35, 42, 52-55, 67, 71

P

paranoid, paranoia, 41, 42, 49, 50, 52, 67
Paranoids The, 59
parody, 21, 23, 24, 26, 27, 36, 43, 44, 67
pastiche, 23. 26. 27. 28
pastoral, 20
Petillon, James, 42, 54
poshlust, 55, 56
Pynchon, Thomas
    Gravity's Rainbow, 63, 64
    Slow Learner, 3
    Vineland 63

Q

Quilty, 21, 22, 23, 26, 27

R

repetition, ix, 27, 32

S

satire, 63
Schlovsky, Victor, ix-xii, 48
signifier, 15, 16, 17, 52, 60, 61
Simmons, Phillip, 63, 64, 65, 67
Sorfa, David, 50, 51, 53
Spiegel, Alan, 63, 66
Stark, John O, 10, 22, 25, 26

T

Tanner, Tony, 43
Trilling, Lionel, 34
Tyson, Lois, 61

U

uncanny, uncanniness, 7, 8, 9, 17, 22, 24, 26, 43, 48, 60, 62
underworld, 19-21

V

voyeur, 62

W

Waugh, Patricia, 51, 52, 61, 66
wild west, western, 26, 17, 22
Williams, William Carlos, vii
Wood, Michael, 25, 34
Wyllie, Barbara, 15

ABOUT THE AUTHOR

MELISSA KARMEN LAM is a graduate of McGill and Canterbury universities and is currently on faculty at the English Department, Chinese University of Hong Kong. She specializes in Contemporary Literature, and is currently working on her next book project on the subject of Chinese Magical Realism and the Asian Diaspora.

Among other works, Melissa Lam is the author of many articles including 'Lolita: Inventing a World through Language', Blunt Constructions: The Cultural Ghosting of Métis in Canada and 'Diasporic Literature: The Politics of Identity and Language'. In 2004–2005 she was cofounder of the Defect Perfection Literary journal published by the University of Canterbury, New Zealand.

Melissa Lam is also an independent visual arts Curator and publishes frequently in magazines such as *Vie Des Arts, The Art Newspaper, Asia Art News and Sculpture Magazine*. She is the author of 'Zhang Huan: Altered States', 'Dennis Oppenheim: Revisiting Old Hunting Grounds', and 'Female Curators: From Marcia Tucker to Alana Heiss'.

www.ingramcontent.com/pod-product-compliance
Lightning Source LLC
Chambersburg PA
CBHW021834300426
44114CB00009BA/442